VAN HALEN

at
50

MARTIN POPOFF

CONTENTS

INTRODUCTION

It's one of the great "Where were you?" moments in rock 'n' roll history, especially for guitarists—namely, "Where were you when you first heard 'Eruption'?" Over the years, I've had many axe-slingers talk to me about Eddie, and for every one of them, "Eruption" demanded a response, whether it was to lay the guitar down and never touch it again or to try harder, beginning with figuring out how to tap (which, to the delight of many, wasn't that hard).

As for myself, I was a drummer, but that wasn't what informed my absorption of the *Van Halen* album in 1978. It was more the fact that my buds and I were crazy, knocked-out heavy metal experts by fifteen, which didn't take much because there wasn't much. Essentially in one fell swoop, this baby band had a buzz as the only consortium in the heavy metal universe as good as Judas Priest, with the bonus being that they were American, which was unexpected by this point. The best stuff all came from Britain, even if America had its fun in '76 and '77 with Kiss and Ted Nugent and Aerosmith, and here come some guys delivering the goods on their first record but not so relentlessly that they pulled away from the pack. That's the thing—and I remember it clear as day—"On Fire," "I'm the One," "Ain't Talkin' 'bout Love," and "Atomic Punk" formed a suite that left us wanting more, but the rest of the album . . . fairly regular-issue stuff.

And then we're into every Van Halen album as a new release, with that sense of anticipation and curiosity leading up to the launch. And then upon arrival, damn it, again, there was never enough to grab hold of, especially if you were an angry headbanger. Van Halen showed up casual, their attention wandered, and then they barely stuck around anyway, daring to put in the racks the shortest albums in the business. The arrival of this year's record always had an element of prank to it, but you took it in good fun, because you could tell Dave, Eddie, Michael, and Alex were having fun. And besides, they kept winning, carrying on like the most natural place for them was at the top of a sunny hillock looking down, speaking with you for five minutes, and then running off to drive a fast car, skydive, mountain-climb, shotgun beers, or something.

The first stop of the reunion tour with Sammy, at the Coliseum in Greensboro, North Carolina, June 11, 2004

All that action, along with the darker dramas (we found out that it wasn't always fun), made the construction of this book nearly as fun by proxy, or at least 3 percent as fun, because who lives life better than Van Halen? Accentuating the experience—all the giddiness, the creative madness, and the tragedy—was the format of the book. The mandate was to pick and then write about fifty career milestones or highlights in the band's history, whether they be tiger-print sports jacket on the emotional rainbow or black funeral formal and everything in between, including no shirt, no shorts, no service. And I can't take credit for the format: That's all the doing of my beloved publisher Motorbooks, who have stacked a number of titles in this series, three of which they've asked me to do thus far, on AC/DC, Kiss, and David Bowie (the last of which was an "at 75").

Sticking with tradition, every studio and official live album gets an entry, and in Van Halen's case, that means twelve and two, respectively. That leaves more than enough room for "all" the proper compilations as well, of which there are a ludicrous two. It's like the pranking continues, with none of that adding up

to what millions of fans around the world would have loved from this explosive band, one that second lead singer Sammy Hagar consistently says was the best band in the world. Which is pretty sensible: It's remarkable when a four-piece can have two hugely distinct and chopsy musicians among the ranks, along with the amusing narrative that they happen to be brothers. Then there's Michael Anthony, consummate bassist and surprise weapon at the microphone, an unrealized lead singer in his own right. David Lee Roth and Sammy Hagar are both titans at their positions, and then even Gary Cherone and Wolfgang Van Halen are top operators in the biz as well.

But yes, twelve studio albums across thirty-four years is just a cryin' shame, but if we can look on the bright side, there was a lot of playing live, including the four years before they got a record out. More of a cryin' shame is the breakdowns in relations, most saliently between the brothers and the lead singers, with Michael caught in the middle, although he caused his own problems by not participating enough in the songwriting.

And then most distressing of all was watching Eddie go through cancer and then, on October 6, 2020, dying from it. A world without this life-affirming and life-giving band, symbolized by Eddie's smile as he shredded, just didn't seem to make sense and still doesn't, much the way Neil Peart's death earlier that year turned the progressive rock world upside down. Both were youthful, at sixty-five and sixty-seven, seemingly with so much more music in them.

Fortunately for the world of art—subset music, subset rock 'n' roll, subset guitaring—Eddie Van Halen left us with a wall-heaving and made heavy with his magic, sitting there at his home studio, 5150. As the fantasy of so many of us lifelong Van Halen fans goes, a next chapter of Van Halen is still to be written. I suppose this book is a modest chapter itself, but what the fans really want is for Wolfgang to sift and lift from those tapes and build us another Van Halen album and then another. While Dave, Sammy, Michael, and Uncle Alex are still with us and able (and various degrees of willing), it's not an impossibility.

Okay, enough fantasizing. He's spoken on the subject and has kind of dismissed it—at least for now. In that light, we must console ourselves in that we have the sacred texts, those twelve studio albums, and now you have an epilogue to the canon, with the hopes that upon reading *Van Halen at 50*, you'll turn back to the records and relive the insane musical chemistry and glory of a band on fire across those dozen documents.

Standing on top of the world, Cobo Hall, Detroit, April 5, 1984

Act One
DIAMOND DAVE

Fair Warning–era
Van Halen, 1981.
From left: Alex, Eddie,
Dave, and Michael

1

01
SINNER'S SWING!
VAN HALEN IS BORN

Like Axl Rose, David Lee Roth grew up in Indiana. But unlike Rose, who grew up under horrible broken-home circumstances, David grew up the son of an ophthalmologist and a teacher, had a couple of sisters, and later combined his "can do" attitude with his salt-of-the-earth upbringing in the Midwest. Still, he was a California golden boy busting to get out, so it was serendipitous that in his teens, the family would move to Pasadena, inland eleven miles from downtown Los Angeles, the media-mad machine that thrives on characters like Diamond Dave.

Also in Pasadena were the brothers Van Halen, Alex and Edward, who moved to the area in 1962 from the Netherlands. Instantly musical—father Jan was a skilled pianist, saxophonist, and clarinetist—they both started on piano, after which Alex began playing the guitar and Eddie, younger by two years, began on the drums. They'd soon switch and then advance rapidly, winding up in their first band together, the Broken Combs, while still in elementary school—Eddie was all but nine years old. All the while, the boys were slowly picking up English, learning in a segregated school, and being bullied as foreigners.

Soon came the psychedelic rock era, and Eddie was transformed by the guitar playing of Cream's Eric Clapton, cadging all his solos note for note without learning how to read music, a method he had already set upon through his rote memorization of classical pieces for the piano. Early inspiration also came from Jimi Hendrix, The Who, Black Sabbath, Mountain, and Cactus, particularly that band's rendition of "Parchman Farm."

Getting together with a bass player called Dennis Travis and then Mark Stone, the guys progressed through bands like The Trojan Rubber Company and Genesis, eventually arriving at the heavy name of Mammoth. In a story redolent of the way Blue Öyster Cult got Eric Bloom, they had been renting a PA system for $35 a night from a guy they knew well but couldn't stand—namely, David Lee Roth, ex-singer of a rival band called Red Ball Jet, now long dissolved with their lead singer drifting, practicing his acoustic guitar, and plotting his next move. Eddie had his hands full in Mammoth, playing guitar as well as lead singing (they also had a keyboard player), as he puts it, screaming like Kurt Cobain and losing his voice halfway through their sets. Dave had auditioned and failed fantastically a couple times (as far back as 1971), but by August 1973, he had ingratiated himself into the ranks, with Eddie, Alex, and Mark calculating that now they wouldn't have to pay for PA rental.

Next, they changed their name to Van Halen, and soon after Mark Stone was replaced by Michael Anthony, with the guys entering the summer of 1974 as the classic lineup that would conquer the world. Dave claims that the name switch from Mammoth was his idea, citing the timeless, long-term, non-pigeonholed marketing possibilities of "Van Halen," akin to Santana. Eddie readily agreed, finding the new name epic. Confirming the concept was the recent release of *Montrose* by Ronnie Montrose, Sammy Hagar, Bill Church, and Denny Carmassi. Produced by Ted Templeman, that band's self-titled debut landed like an atomic bomb, living on in legend as the sort of blueprint to Van Halen's own first album to drop with equal force five years later.

Eddie's early inspiration came from many corners. The Long Island band Cactus was a notable influence, particularly their take on the old blues chestnut "Parchman Farm."

02
COULD THIS BE MAGIC?
GENE SIMMONS AND PAUL STANLEY DISCOVER VAN HALEN

Paul and Gene perform their good cop/bad cop routine, New York City.

By the summer of 1976, Van Halen were firing on all cylinders, playing Gazzari's regularly. The new rival band (besides Quiet Riot, featuring Randy Rhoads) was called The Boyz, featuring George Lynch. This is actually whom Gene Simmons and Paul Stanley had gone to see that fateful night, November 2, 1976, at the Starwood in West Hollywood. Turns out Stanley and Simmons had seen the band before, in makeup doing their Kiss set, and this was them promising that they had originals too and were worth signing. The Boyz went on first and had a bum night. Stanley and Simmons were backstage talking to them when, all of a sudden, Van Halen fired up. Quickly begging off, the Kiss legends made their way back to the VIP balcony to watch the set, all the while the crowd craning around to see if they could spot their heroes sans makeup.

Simmons and Stanley were impressed enough to whisk Van Halen away to Village Recorders right after their set to record a demo deep into the night. They managed about ten songs with Simmons presiding, including "On Fire," "Runnin' with the Devil," "Somebody Get Me a Doctor," and "House of Pain," which Simmons found particularly powerful. There was also "Put Out the Lights," which became "Beats Workin'" on 2012's *A Different Kind of Truth*. Also making it to the band's last record would be "Big River," changed to "Big Trouble"; "Let's Get Rockin'," changed to "Outta Space"; and "She's the Woman," which retained the original title. Simmons had also signed them to his production company, Man of 1000 Faces, put together as an entrepreneurial side venture to start working with other bands.

Further recording, mostly overdubs, was done at Electric Lady Studios in New York City, with the band hopeful that this was going to be their big break. The trip to New York also served as a showcase for Kiss manager Bill Aucoin, who wasn't impressed with the band, taking a particular dislike to David Lee Roth and going so far as to say he could see working with the band but they'd need to replace the singer. Interestingly, this opinion had lined up with what so many club-goers had been saying in '75 and '76—that Dave's Jim Dandy act was dated and holding the band back from the greatness they deserved. Simmons claims that the demo, now bulged to about fifteen tracks and mixed by Dave Wittman, didn't do much for Stanley either. Also along the way, Simmons suggested the guys change their name to Daddy Longlegs.

As Simmons puts it, the response of Aucoin, along with the fact that Kiss was about to get very busy with their *Rock and Roll Over* tour, prompted him to "rip up the contract," freeing Van Halen to check out other options. The turn of events was hugely embarrassing for Eddie, who resumed his clubbing duties back in Los Angeles, loath to talk about what happened with even the closest of friends and indeed further working to keep the story out of the news as if it had never happened.

Van Halen rocks Hollywood's Sunset Strip in 1976.

03

HEAR ABOUT IT LATER

TED TEMPLEMAN AND MO OSTIN CHECK OUT THE BAND AT THE STARWOOD

Bruised by their failure with the Kiss camp, along with mounting rejections as they shopped their Gene Simmons demo, Van Halen went back to work trying to make Van Halen work. But opportunity would soon knock again. Marshall Berle, nephew of Milton Berle, who had been booking acts for the Whisky a Go Go in West Hollywood, had called up the Warner Bros. offices, recommending to his friend Ted Templeman that he check out Van Halen when they played the Starwood the following month. Templeman bit and went by himself to the band's poorly attended show on February 2, 1977. He was immediately taken with Eddie Van Halen, likening his style and chops and casual manner to the greats of the jazz world. Plus, the band played the club like it was a stadium. Weak link: David Lee Roth, who couldn't sing and looked awkward.

The band was there again the next night, and this time Templeman brought producer and Warner VP Russ Titelman and CEO Mo Ostin, specifically going to the top because (a) Ostin was powerful enough to sign the band on the spot and (b) he liked his hard rock. Templeman also knew that Ostin would appreciate the band's cover of The Kinks' "You Really Got Me." The three of them, along with Marshall Berle, watched Van Halen from the VIP area. After the show, they went backstage and met with the band, complimenting them on "You Really Got Me," which Ostin had been instrumental in making a hit in America. Ostin asked Berle if the band had a manager, to which Berle said no. Ostin then appointed Berle as Van Halen's new manager.

Then and there a letter of intent was drawn up, but the guys acted all businesslike and said they'd think about it before signing it the next day at Warner's Burbank offices, with formal contracts to follow on March 3, exactly a month after the showcase.

But the narrative continues: What do we do with Dave? Before the end of the month, Templeman and engineer Donn Landee had the band at Sunset Recorders making demos, and things weren't improving. The music was as magical as it was live, with the band tracking twenty-five songs in three hours. Templeman was particularly impressed with how Eddie did double duty, blazing through his solos and then switching back to rhythm all in one go. It's something Eddie wanted to retain when they made the actual record, this idea of being a one-guitar power trio and (usually) not putting a rhythm track behind his solos. But the reservations Templeman and Titelman and Ostin had about Dave persisted. They conferred and almost suggested to Eddie that they put in a call to Sammy Hagar to replace Dave. Donn Landee agreed.

But then in the same amusing manner that Dave ingratiated himself with the Van Halens, given an inch and taking a mile, he charmed Templeman just enough to where he'd get doled, in bits and pieces, the coaching he needed to catch up to the rest of the band. It must be said here that Michael Anthony was serious as well, getting top gear and working hard. Before they knew it, they were recording Van Halen's first album, and there would be no looking back.

★★★★★★★★★★★★★★★★★★★★★★★★★
NON-TRANSFERABLE · NOT FOR RESALE
COMPLIMENTARY ADMISSION · NOT VALID AFTER 10:30 P.M.

Saturday, April 30th

V A N   H A L E N

FAREWELL CONCERT

STARWOOD

8151 SANTA MONICA BLVD. (at Crescent Heights) in Hollywood
DOORS OPEN 8:00 P.M. · 656-2200 · NO AGE LIMIT

04
I'M THE ONE

VAN HALEN ISSUE GROUNDBREAKING DEBUT ALBUM

Ted Templeman and engineer Donn Landee had Van Halen back at Sunset in September to record what would later be considered one of the best debut albums ever recorded, Van Halen: *Van Halen*, the album so good they hadda name it twice.

The methodology wasn't that much different from the demo sessions. The band would play live a handful of times and then pick the best take. Dave's singing on the live blow was politely tolerated, as was the odd flub from Alex, even if Eddie would be the first to give his brother hell, the main cause of tension to the sessions. There'd be the odd overdub, like the famed car horn at the beginning of "Runnin' with the Devil" and a doubling with Coral electric sitar during Eddie's "Ain't Talkin' 'bout Love" solo. Templeman also loved the "youthful" harmony backing vocals the guys could do, because it reminded him of The Beach Boys.

But there were more serious overdubs too. Once the musicians were done with their parts, they'd be sent home, with Templeman, Landee, and the lead singer left to do some additional work. As Templeman puts it, he really didn't want Eddie, Alex, and Michael to see how much of a struggle it was getting performances out of Dave that weren't flat, pitchy, or, as the night wore on, hoarse. All three would be drained, with Dave's confidence fragile, but in the end, it would be worth it.

Beyond this album's sales and reputation as quickly and forevermore insanely iconic, the singing on it is, too. Consider it anecdotal proof if you like, but this author has probably heard a couple hundred people talk about *Van Halen* in some detail, and there's not been a single eyebrow raised at the vocals. In fact, people love what Dave does all over it nearly as much as what Eddie does.

And one of the things Eddie does is "Eruption." Templeman recalls how he heard Eddie playing it one day and asked what it was. Eddie responded that it was nothing more than a warm-up exercise. Landee had already been a step ahead of Templeman and had hit the record button. Within ten minutes of Templeman hearing what is unarguably considered the most famous solo electric guitar piece of all time, the take we'd hear on the album was recorded. And it was the only take. Eddie requested that he be allowed to do it again, and Templeman said no—something that haunts the producer to this day.

As for the rest of the album, well, *Van Halen* was the most ferocious hard rock verging on heavy metal album to come out of America possibly ever as of its February 10, 1978, release. It's more distortion pedal- and riff-mad than *Rocks*, *Ted Nugent*, or *Struck Down* from Yesterday and Today, even if it's only marginally more intense than *Montrose*, also produced by Templeman and Landee. And then, as alluded to earlier, positively Scorpions- and Judas Priest–level are the likes of "Ain't Talkin' 'bout Love," "I'm the One," "Atomic Punk," and "On Fire."

In that mid-zone but delivering significant slabs of hard rock to the radio masses are "Runnin' with the Devil" and "Jamie's Cryin'"—both sober, measured, and thus mature and starry—and then the band's molten cover of "You Really Got Me," which was generally sent over the airways with "Eruption" strapped to the front of it like a bottle rocket, as it is on the record. "Feel Your Love Tonight" and "Little Dreamer" haven't aged well, but the band's cover of John Brim's "Ice Cream Man," essentially a boogie-woogie '50s rocker, has aged just fine, delivering that Diamond Dave humor we all know and love.

The impact of the *Van Halen* album was immediate. The subtitle of Greg Renoff's excellent formation-days book, *Van Halen Rising*, says it all: *How a Southern California Backyard Party Band Saved Heavy Metal*. Essentially, the album was

plunged into a void in hard rock on both sides of the pond like a mythical sword into a boulder. Led Zeppelin, Black Sabbath, Deep Purple, Uriah Heep, Aerosmith, Kiss, Ted Nugent . . . all were faltering or gone. Nor was there yet significant success coming from the second guard likes of UFO, Thin Lizzy, Scorpions, Rush, Judas Priest, or Rainbow.

In this light, Van Halen, most notably with the debut but with the next couple of albums as well, would serve as creative and commercial connective tissue toward the New Wave of British Heavy Metal en route to the massive hard rock resurgence represented in the main by hair metal. In fact, all forms of heavy rock would do glorious business clear through to the early '90s, and we would be remiss in not citing the excitement around Van Halen—and Eddie Van Halen in particular—for getting hard-charged guitar rock to the place of prominence it enjoyed throughout the '80s. We might add that most of the impact would be felt right in Van Halen's backyard, almost as if the band had flyered the city and then pulled off their biggest and beeriest backyard party yet.

Van Halen

If you haven't heard them yet, it's not their fault.

Van Halen has been making a lot of noise since their album was released 4 months ago. California's hardest-rocking band has placed 3 scorching singles on the radio, earned reviews comparing them to Zeppelin and Aerosmith, and destroyed audiences from coast to coast.

Turn on a radio or talk to a friend. Then you'll know why everyone's excited about Van Halen.

VAN HALEN. Featuring the singles 'You Really Got Me,' 'Runnin' With The Devil,' and 'Jamie's Crying.'

Produced by Ted Templeman

On Warner Bros. records and tapes.

From the Warner Bros. Album BSK 3075 VAN HALEN

VAN HALEN
Produced by Ted Templeman
Engineered by Donn Landee

PROMO-TION

NOT FOR SALE

MONO

WBS 8707
(VCA 7322)

3:47

Van Halen Music
ASCAP

AIN'T TALKIN' 'BOUT LOVE
Van Halen/Alex Van Halen/
(Edward Van Halen/David Lee Roth/
Michael Anthony)

05
GET UP
THE BAND EMBARKS ON FIRST TOUR

Supporting Montrose and headliner Journey at the Palladium, New York City, March 25, 1978

Like a shot rocket, on their very first tour, Van Halen burst out of California and onto the world stage, notching a lifetime's worth of experience over an epic ten-month, 174-date campaign that would set their path for life. The band did a few local shows before playing their first legitimate tour date, March 3, 1978, in the five-thousand-plus-capacity Aragon Ballroom, far from home in Chicago. The first leg was in support of Ronnie Montrose as a solo act, touring his *Open Fire* album, and Journey, who, before the tour was through, would resort to sabotaging Van Halen's PA because they were too good.

Next came a handful of mainland European dates, followed by a U.K. support slot with Black Sabbath, beginning May 16 in Sheffield, England. Typical of Sabbath's dumb luck at this time, Ozzy Osbourne, realizing how spent his band was and stung by recently having support band Kiss do them one better, requested that they find a "a bar band from LA" to support them. He knew they were in trouble once he saw "Eruption" live. He even called David Lee Roth "the best-looking man in the world." Eventually he conceded that Van Halen should be headlining the tour, while also remembering and ruing the days when Boston quickly outshone the Sabs back in 1976 on that band's self-titled debut album, which even eclipsed what Van Halen would manage with their own first record. Tony Iommi was less impressed with Eddie, taking him aside at one point and telling him to stop copying his moves. A week into the tour, the band received the news that their album had gone gold.

A typical set list found Van Halen playing the entire first album along with liberal individual solos, uncommon for an opener. When that was done, they'd encore with "D.O.A." and "Bottoms Up!" which no one had heard yet. Occasionally there would be trial balloons like "Voodoo Queen," "Last Night," "Down in Flames," and "Somebody Get Me a Doctor," but generally the point was to hammer home the band's hit album.

Incredibly, a mere six months after the release of their debut album, Van Halen found themselves playing a half-dozen dates in Japan, after which it was straight into the Texxas Jam festival and an intensive American tour (plus Vancouver; on the first leg, they had played Toronto) clear through to the end of September. Once again, for the most part, Black Sabbath was the kicking post, supporting the ill-received *Never Say Die* record. Along the way, with the *Van Halen* album on steady ascendance, the band was starting to headline their own fill-in shows, with many of these chaotic affairs making for some of the best memories of the relentless 1978 campaign.

In October, it was back to Europe, once more supporting Black Sabbath, who, by this point, were becoming gluttons for punishment, too tired to fight back. Truth is, Eddie and the guys were respectful enough, having covered "Tomorrow's Dream" of all songs, back in the club days. More shows with Sabbath were notched on a third U.S. tour leg, commencing November 3 in St. Petersburg, Florida, and continuing to December 3 in San Diego. So concluded a jam-packed year of what they call "blowing away the headliner," with Van Halen doing the deed over and over again. There would be no question that the next tour would find the band headlining.

06

SUMMER NIGHTS

VAN HALEN PLAY TEXXAS JAM

Fighting the effects of a long Pan Am flight from Japan, Van Halen were about to put another notch on their tour-themed bullet belt, this time playing a massive stadium gig on July 1, 1978. The event was the inaugural Texxas Jam (officially the Texxas World Music Festival) at the Cotton Bowl in Dallas, Texas, secured by Aerosmith and Ted Nugent manager David Krebs to showcase his acts at the top of a big bill. Van Halen faced additional hardship for their show when most of their equipment had been shipped to Chicago by mistake, with the band having to play on rented and borrowed gear—fortunately, Eddie had some guitars, which he was allowed to carry onto the plane.

Still they triumphed, on a day of 104°F heat, as part of a bill that included Walter Egan (who directly preceded Van Halen), Eddie Money, Atlanta Rhythm Section, Head East, Heart, Cheech and Chong, Frank Marino and Mahogany Rush (also a Leber Krebs act), their old sparring partners Journey, and the aforementioned Ted Nugent and Aerosmith, both at the height of their fame. The success of the show, attracting one hundred thousand fans despite it being the hottest day of the decade thus far—Van Halen played to about eighty-two thousand—resulted in Texxas Jam being a recurring event in one form or another. Of note, it was the first show of this size in Texas since the ZZ Top hoedown in 1974 when the field at The University of Texas at Austin had been greatly damaged, resulting in a ban of such gatherings.

As for the set list that scorching day, Van Halen opened with their usual two heavy metal rippers "On Fire" and "I'm the One," followed by a bass solo. Next came "Runnin' with the Devil" and the debut album's other metal number, "Atomic Punk," followed by a drum solo. Then they went with lower-temperature deep album tracks "Little Dreamer" and "Feel Your Love

At the ready with Alex's refreshments

TEXXAS WORLD MUSIC FESTIVAL '79
TEXXAS JAM '79
STARRING
BOSTON • HEART
VAN HALEN

Nº 69815

SATURDAY
JUNE
9
1979
SHOWTIME 1:00 PM

COTTON BOWL
DALLAS, TEXAS

$15.00 ADVANCE
GENERAL
ADMISSION
• ADMIT ONE •
NO REFUNDS • NO EXCHANGES

GOOD THIS DATE ONLY | RAIN OR SHINE
PLEASE RETAIN TICKET STUB

Nº 69815

TEXXAS JAM '79
STARRING
BOSTON • HEART
VAN HALEN

COTTON BOWL
DALLAS, TEXAS

SAT., JUNE 9, 1979

$15.00 ADVANCE
GENERAL
ADMISSION
• ADMIT ONE •
NO REFUNDS-NO EXCHANGES

GOOD THIS DATE ONLY
NOT GOOD FOR ADMISSION
IF THIS STUB IS DETACHED

Dave is most definitely
an outdoor cat.

Tonight," following up with "Ain't Talkin' 'bout Love," transitioning into an extended version of "Eruption." Next-record song "D.O.A." and Kinks cover "You Really Got Me" closed the set, with the band getting in "Bottoms Up!," another next-album track, as an encore.

But Texxas Jam was only one of a number of memorable large shows that were to come fast and furious. Two weeks later, Van Halen would be supporting The Rolling Stones and The Doobie Brothers in New Orleans. Then there was Summer Jam and Mississippi River Jam. Finally, on July 23, Van Halen were part of one of Bill Graham's storied Day on the Green bills, along with Foreigner, The Pat Travers Band, headliners Aerosmith, and new hotshots AC/DC, whom Eddie greatly respected and almost feared. A few more jams later, it was back to regular tour duties, with Van Halen essentially hitting every high watermark in terms of touring barely six months after the release of their first album.

Van Halen would return the following year supporting the *II* album and then again in 1986, where they'd headline over Dio, Loverboy, Krokus, Keel, and Bachman-Turner Overdrive. They'd play the last ostensibly Texxas Jam date ever as part of the 1988 Monsters of Rock tour, headlining over Steve Leber/David Krebs act Scorpions, as well as Dokken, Kingdom Come, and Metallica.

TEXXAS STATE FAIRGROUNDS
COTTON BOWL DALLAS, TEXXAS
JUNE 30 — JULY 4

JULY 1 — TEXXAS JAM *
Aerosmith   Ted Nugent
Atlanta Rhythm Section   Head East   Heart
Frank Marino & Mahogany Rush   Eddie Money   Van Halen

JULY 3 — WILLIE NELSON'S ANNUAL PICNIC *
Starring
Willie Nelson   Waylon Jennings   Kris Kristofferson
Jessi Colter   Rita Coolidge
The Charlie Daniels Band   Emmylou Harris
Ray Wylie Hubbard   Billie Swan

JUNE 30 — JULY 4 — THE TEXXAS MUSIC FAIR *

Rock & Roll Midway Rides, Games, Prizes!
Battle Of the Bands   Arts And Crafts Fair
Rock & Roll Supermarket Stereo Shop, Record Store, Novelties!
Indoor Movie Theatres
Flea Market, Food Fair
Skateboard Exhibitions   Livestock Exhibit
Fireworks Display (Nightly)   Laser Show (July 1)
AND MUCH, MUCH MORE

002924

GATE 1 OR 8
JULY 1/2 1978

TEXXAS
WORLD MUSIC FESTIVAL
DAY 1
STARRING
AEROSMITH • TED NUGENT
COTTON BOWL
DALLAS, TEXAS
JULY 1 — SATURDAY
RAIN OR SHINE — 10:00 AM
VALUE: $10.00

TEXXAS
WORLD MUSIC FESTIVAL
DAY 2
STARRING
AEROSMITH • TED NUGENT
COTTON BOWL
DALLAS, TEXAS
JULY 2 — SUNDAY
RAIN OR SHINE — 10:00 AM
VALUE: $10.00
MUST RETAIN THIS PORTION
OF TICKET

$20.00 SERIES

GATE 1 OR 8
002924
TEXXAS WORLD
MUSIC FEST.

$20.00 TOTAL

SERIES PRICE
002924
JULY 1/2 1978

07
EVERYBODY WANTS SOME!!
VAN HALEN CERTIFIED PLATINUM

Producer Ted Templeman and Warner Bros. chairman Mo Ostin join the boys for a picture celebrating Van Halen *II* going gold, Los Angeles, March 23, 1979.

The band was in the United Kingdom on May 24, 1978, when they got news that the Recording Industry Association of America had bestowed upon *Van Halen* its gold certification, for sales of over half a million copies. They were in Aberdeen, Scotland, when they got the news (in advance by a couple days) and recall celebrating in their hotel lobby. Eddie found some gold paint and proceeded to paint the walls gold, resulting in the hotel calling the police.

They were in Germany on October 10, 1978, when the album officially went platinum for a million pancakes served, although it had already been announced in Billboard at the end of September that the band had surpassed that plateau. Manager Marshall Berle commemorated the event by getting the band necklaces with Van Halen logos made out of platinum. Two weeks later, he had his uncle Milton Berle emceeing a party at The Body Shop, a strip club on the Sunset Strip, in honor of the band. In attendance were Stevie Nicks, Bonnie Raitt, and other industry people like KROQ's Rodney Bingenheimer.

Given how record company contracts work, Van Halen, through general excess as well as delinquency on the road that nearly got them kicked off the Black Sabbath tour twice, had racked up over $1 million in debt to the label, with Alex figuring it was closer to $2 million. But that didn't stop the wild celebration at The Body Shop, with Dave and Michael both taking a (clothed) turn on the stripper pole. As a news report noted, "On hand were several of The Body Shop's more comely employees."

Also in celebration of this milestone, Warner Bros. issued "Ain't Talkin' 'bout Love" as the fourth single from the record, a bold move given the squarely heavy metal nature of the song at a time when hard rock was out of vogue and even punk was giving way to the more milquetoast "new wave." In fact, given how alone Van Halen were at being so loud and noisy at the time, you'd have to chalk up the success of the album due to a universal agreement about its high quality, to the point where the obstacle of the distasteful oeuvre they were working in was essentially overcome. In other words, despite the masses putting up violent resistance, Van Halen made them surrender to the charms of heavy metal.

In the history of squarely rock debut albums, only *Boston* went platinum faster than *Van Halen*, getting there in three months compared with eight. Neither *Black Sabbath* nor *Led Zeppelin* reached that certification level that fast, although *Van Halen* was later matched (give a week or two) by both Guns N' Roses with *Appetite for Destruction* and Pearl Jam with *Ten*. It's all great company, and what's perhaps more important, *Van Halen* is arguably cited more than any of those as being the greatest debut album of all time.

Celebrating *Van Halen* going platinum at the Body Shop, Hollywood, California, October 1978

Eddie shows Detroit his tapping technique, March 10, 1978.

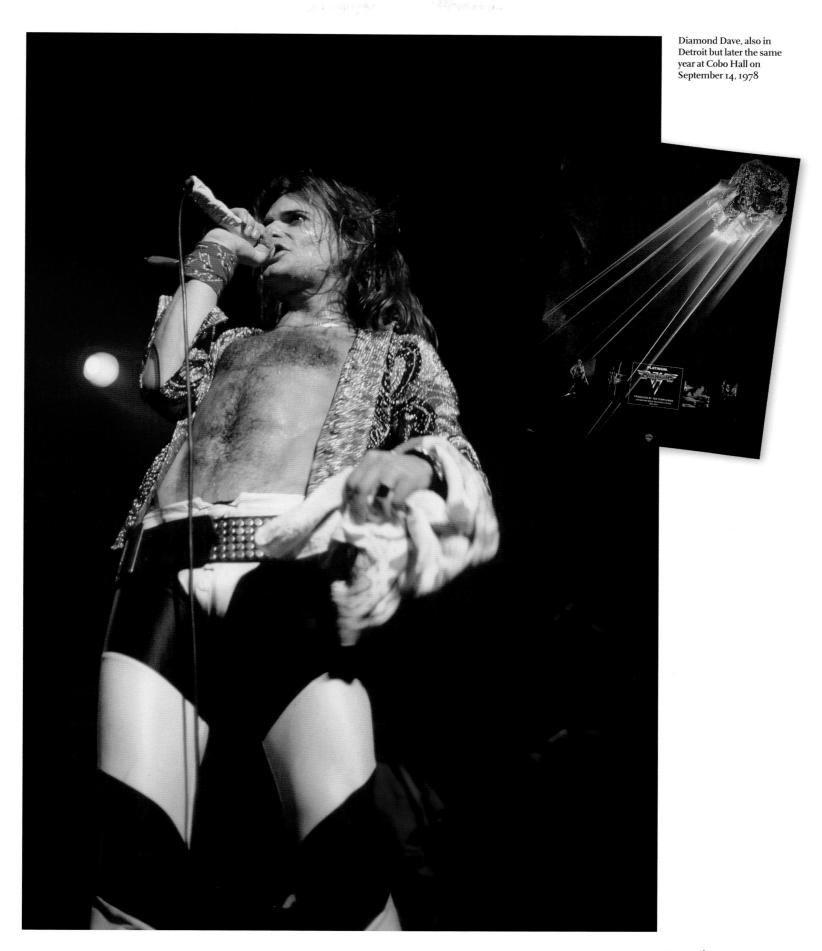

Diamond Dave, also in
Detroit but later the same
year at Cobo Hall on
September 14, 1978

EDDIE VAN HALEN: KING OF THE TAPPERS

There's the brown sound, there's his propensity to solo without backing rhythm track, there's his leap to licks at every opportunity (like a drummer to his toms), but more than anything, definitive of Eddie as a guitarist is his use of the tapping technique.

So what's tapping? Well, it's essentially the idea of making the string on a stringed instrument vibrate, or make a sound, by tapping directly down on top of it, either with a bare finger or with a pick, in a sort of collision with the frets. Directly related, or on a gray scale with this, is the idea of hammer-ons and pull-offs. One can use the fretting hand essentially as a capo or movable nut and then tap with the right at any place on the fretboard. There's also single-handed tapping, two-handed tapping, and tapped harmonics, which can be heard on "Dance the Night Away" and "Women in Love." There's also a showmanship element to tapping: It's pretty cool seeing a guitarist put both hands on the neck, and indeed, one can also put one or both hands over the top of the neck for added flash.

Eddie isn't the first to tap, but in terms of both quantity and quality, he's overwhelmed all comers. It's been done on violin (notably by Niccolò Paganini), acoustic guitar, and other acoustic instruments going back to ancient Turkey. There's ukulele player Roy Smeck as well as Jimmie Webster, Merle Travis, Vittorio Camardese, and George Van Eps.

The history in terms of rock includes the likes of Steve Hackett from Genesis and Harvey Mandel from Canned Heat, whom both Eddie and Dokken's George Lynch caught live at the Starwood. Mandel cites his partner in Pure Food and Drug Act, Randy Resnick, in terms of where he himself got it from. There's also Emmett Chapman, inventor of the Chapman Stick, and Dave Bunker, who pioneered the touch guitar. Larry Carlton taps on Steely Dan's "Kid Charlemagne," as does Carlos Santana on "Hope You're Feeling Better."

Closer to Eddie, Billy Gibbons is often cited as Eddie's first inspiration; but then again, there are occasional taps in the work of Duane Allman, Frank Zappa, Ace Frehley, Brian May, Glenn Tipton, and Leslie West, all of whom Eddie would have been aware of. But direct from Eddie himself comes the recollection that he saw Jimmy Page tap on "Heartbreaker" back in 1971 at the Forum, creating a triplet pattern with his fretting hand as he raised his right hand over his head in a demonstration of "Look, Ma, one hand."

Ironically, the same day Judas Priest's *Killing Machine* was issued in the United Kingdom, featuring Glenn Tipton tapping quite clearly and elaborately on "Hell Bent for Leather," Van Halen saw the release of their first record. On it, we hear "Eruption," which still stands as the most iconic of tapping demonstration songs. Eddie is using both hands, something pioneered most closely by Steve Hackett, who taps on "Musical Box," "Return of the Giant Hogweed," and "Moonlit Night."

But "Eruption" was not to be a one-off. Eddie would go on to tap like a drummer would do fills, in short bursts and transitions inside of solos, from riffs to solos, as bar-enders, mixed with whammy bar dive-bombs or simply as a form of chirpy, cheery conversation with the listener. Bottom line, he'd quickly build a catalog of tapping passages that utilized every variation of the form, including the two main techniques of one hand versus two.

As interesting outliers, he offers acoustic tapping on "Spanish Fly" and, at the other end, a sort of aggressive slap-tapping on "Mean Street." "Ice Cream Man" mixes tapping with bends and slides, while "Women in Love" demonstrates a pinging, chiming, harmonic, graceful version of the form. For some really great characteristic Eddie tapping during the course of standard meat-and-potatoes electric guitaring, look no further than "You Really Got Me" and "I'm the One." Tapping as artful music making is demonstrated in Eddie's "Jump" solo, where the technique is used sparingly but memorably. It's an example of tapping being a sort of syllable or word in Eddie's vast vocabulary, something effortlessly integrated into the conversation he's having with listeners on these songs within songs. "Source of Infection" from *OU812* is a tapping tour de force, to the point where the guys almost forget to write a proper song and instead create what somewhat sounds like classical music for heavy metal guitar. Also from that album, "Mine All Mine" demonstrates the idea of deliberately tapping just a few notes at a time, here and there, while "A.F.U. (Naturally Wired)" is at the opposite end, with Eddie going nuts, rapid-fire, and atonal.

In the end, Eddie created a legacy that inspired tapping to become a regular part of the toolbox for the class of guitar "shredders" we'd see in the '80s. By demonstrating the concept's versatility and musicality regularly across fully five albums before "hair metal" even began, Eddie cemented his place as tapping's number one go-to guy, influencing the likes of Randy Rhoads, George Lynch, Steve Vai, Joe Satriani, Vinnie Moore, Joe Stump, and Paul Gilbert, who, indeed also by proxy, represent the general idea of the guitar hero industry, which again is a segment of the industry we can attribute pretty much to Eddie all by his lonesome.

Eddie demonstrates his two-handed tapping technique at Madison Square Garden, New York City, March 30, 1984. The band played there the following night as well.

08
THE FULL BUG
VAN HALEN ISSUE THE ROUGH 'N' TUMBLE SECOND ALBUM

Van Halen got smacked with all the clichés about second albums. Uncommon as rock 'n' roll stories go was how good the debut did, although on the flip side, the band was deeply in debt. The guys had flopped back onto their parents' couches (they were still living at home) after an epic ten-month tour and were told to get right back in the studio to deliver another record, with zero time for writing. There was also zero rest, and there'd be zero rest after the album was done either. Plus, they were instructed to make it fast, as Eddie puts it, taking three weeks to make Van Halen *II*, issued March 23, 1979, versus the one week to make the now-platinum debut.

Fortunately, this was a band with a vault full of pretty good songs and worthy but half-baked ideas. As had happened with the first one, the band would draw from their club days material, twisting and turning it into shape, adding waves of confidence gathered from the previous ten months of "it" band status. "Bring on the Girls" would become "Beautiful Girls," but arriving essentially fully formed were the likes of "Somebody Get Me a Doctor," "Bottoms Up!," "Outta Love Again," and "D.O.A." Then there was the cover of "You're No Good," already a hit for Linda Ronstadt in 1975, with the band assuaged by the fact that nobody seemed concerned if Van Halen albums were particularly long. In other words, the preposterous idea of *II* turned out doable, even more so if the band was gonna play loose and free.

That they most definitely did, with *II* sounding significantly less considered and polished against the debut. In fact, as metaphor for this narrative, the opening track is a cover and the opening of the opening track sounds like the band ambling into the room and warming up, with Michael making most of the noise. What ensues is an amusingly nonpurposeful version of "You're No Good," something approaching a piss-take. Turns out, it's not a particularly good song anyway—who knew?

But then things turn around fast, with the guys proving that they should be writing their own material. There'd be fully three selections among the band's own eight songs here that are more melodic and poppier than anything on the debut. "Dance the Night Away" is the most up-tempo of these, and it's a gorgeous proposition, visceral of performance and recording but accessible on radio and to both sexes.

Next is "Somebody Get Me a Doctor," the heavy metal-est of tracks on the album, getting there through a trace of diabolus in musica, of tritone, at the verses, even if the adjoining riff betrays its older writing. The live-feel intensity of the band's performance really comes through, leading one to comparisons with Led Zeppelin and The Who, also four-man power trios. "Bottoms

Perhaps *II* would have sold
more quickly if this was
used for the cover art.

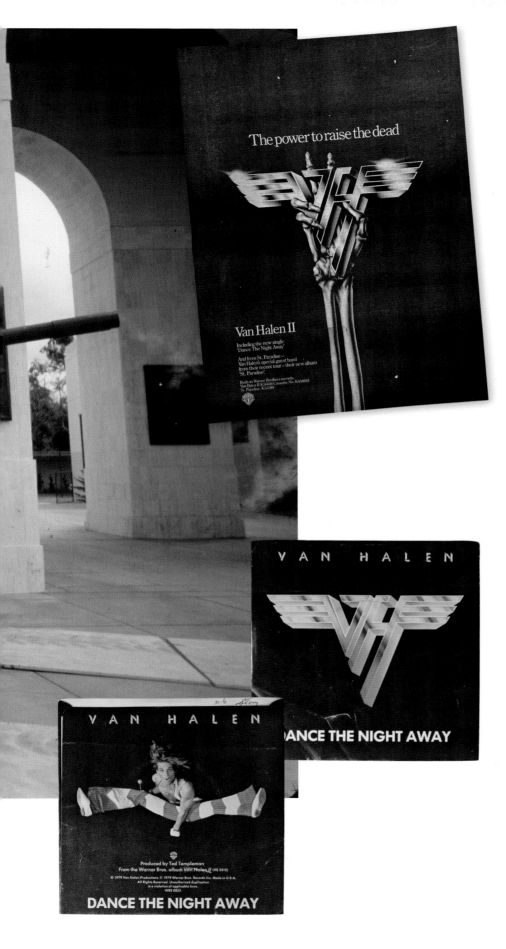

Up!" reprises the shuffle feel of "I'm the One," while "Outta Love Again" showcases the band as daring, rhythmic, noisy, again, living on the edge like The Who circa *Live at Leeds.*

Over to side 2 of the original vinyl, there's a second fully modern heavy metal track in "Light Up the Sky," again, the comparative brashness coming through despite using the same studio, Sunset Recorders, and the same knob-twiddlers in Ted Templeman and Donn Landee. Next comes "Spanish Fly," essentially an acoustic guitar follow-up to "Eruption." While that instrumental piece collapses into "You Really Got Me," "Spanish Fly" gives way to a similar song of chords stacked like pancakes, only this time an original. "D.O.A." features a simple but ornery riff that is relentless, egging on the verses like it eggs on the chorus. All the while Eddie massages in conversational (and howling) licks, playing with the simple setup like it's his last day on earth.

"Women in Love" is pure ridiculous Van Halen, the band writing a ballad and then beating it to a pulp like it's a stadium sound check. It's the perfect setup to the ebullient "Beautiful Girls," which finds the band once again blurring the line between ballad and sunburned heavy metal, managing to evoke images of The Beach Boys somewhere amid the chaos. We must reiterate that these two closing selections, along with "Dance the Night Away," are lighter and happier than anything on the debut. But again, even if the heaviest songs on *II* can't match the firepower of "Atomic Punk" or "On Fire," there's a danger in the devil-may-care delivery from start to finish across *II* that makes it somehow cooler and more underground than the first record.

Back in '79, I remember it feeling like the band was asking us to excuse the mess, but they were tired. But then again, we're all tired together, given the Van Wailin' tornado we'd all just been through. With that request, although everyone loved the first album, we'd find our way to loving the second album, too, despite the cheerful (and perhaps a bit silly) quality of the singles—namely, "Dance the Night Away" and "Beautiful Girls." As a result, *II* certified gold on April 3 and platinum on May 8, reaching #6 on the Billboard charts, with the album currently sitting at five-times-platinum. But the real news was that Van Halen were back on the road as headliners, killin' it in North America but also playing Europe and Japan on what was wryly called the World Vacation Tour, consisting of about seven months of Van Halen mania. Then it was time to do it all over again, with additional demands from the band upon its fans.

09

AND THE CRADLE WILL ROCK . . .

VAN HALEN ISSUE WOMEN AND CHILDREN FIRST

VAN HALEN

Women and Children First

As the band arced and barked their way to a third album, it wasn't exactly all work and no play. Add it up and the band saw fully five months away from the road between the last tour date for *II*, on October 7, 1979, and the first date for *Women and Children First*, on March 19, 1980. For a normal band, one would assume five months of hard studio graft. But for California's favorite punk rock band, if you believe Eddie, the new album was done in six days with an extra two for mixing. Whatever the extent of exaggeration, it was quick, with the band underscoring their firecracker approach across the ensuing interview cycle, sneering at the likes of Fleetwood Mac, Steely Dan, and Foreigner for being boring and making boring records.

Women and Children First, issued on March 26, 1980, was anything but boring. Recording once again with Ted Templeman and Donn Landee at Sunset Sound (a.k.a. Sunset Sound Recorders), the band turned in a blazing, incendiary device of a record, aggressively irreverent of approach, underscored by the deliverance of a side 2 that clocks in at barely over fourteen minutes.

Side 1 of the original vinyl, however, is long enough, and it's wall-to-wall mayhem. Opener "And the Cradle Will Rock . . ." would turn out to be the album's most studied and storied track, not just for the innovative and mangled use of "keyboards" but for its sophisticated chord structure and its sobriety relative to the rest of the record. It would be the album's only single, charting at a modest #55 but slow burning into rock 'n' roll history and consciousness over the decades to the point where it's outlasted many other fine Van Halen songs.

"Everybody Wants Some!!" and "Fools" represent the stompin' and stonkin' core of the album, both of them being little more than jams but winning the game due to chemistry and humidity. "Everybody Wants Some!!" would become a celebrated concert favorite due to its casual-rapping, guitar-howling, tribal-drummed verses that cede way for a payoff of a chorus as magically stadium rock as anything in the catalog. "Fools" gives us a minute of noise before anything happens, and then not much happens other than an up-tempo blues that hints at a shuffle—not surprising, given that the song began surfacing live as far back as 1975. Closing the side is "Romeo Delight," a deep-track favorite of the fans due to its heavy metal nature, its speed, and the dramatic stop/start nature of the song.

Side 2 begins with "Tora! Tora!" a one-minute intro of tritone heavy metal before the guys collapse into the wacky and chaotic "Loss of Control," with origins back to 1977. Southern rock meets speed metal, this one jittery and scattered, aligning with The Who–like sound sculpturing of "Everybody Wants Some!!"

"Take Your Whiskey Home," with roots back to 1974, is another example of an American band clicking and flicking an A/B switch between British blues boom conventions and heavy metal, also something the British did but beginning in the late '60s, versus the Americans, who carried over the idea all the way to the mid-'70s. It's the album's second most studiously assembled song, after the opener, and as a result, it also shows up regularly on classic rock radio. Next comes "Could This Be

Women and Children First went platinum within a couple months of issue, en route to its current triple-platinum status, albeit with the last attempts by management at certification now going back thirty years.

DJ Lee Roth, at WLUP
radio, Chicago, October
27, 1980

WELL, THEY SAID ANYTHING COULD HAPPEN.

VAN HALEN
Women and Children First
The New Album Also available on cassette.

Magic?," a squarely bluegrass song in the tradition of similar Led Zeppelin excursions, notably on *III* and *Physical Graffiti*. In the lexicon of Van Halen, it's partway from "Ice Cream Man" to "Big Bad Bill (Is Sweet William Now)" and "Happy Trails." But yes, at a symbolic level, it aligns Van Halen with the daring and derring-do of the greats like Queen and Led Zeppelin and, in an American orbit, Aerosmith, with songs like "Big Ten Inch Record."

The album closes with "In a Simple Rhyme," another song of many on the album that skirts the edges of southern rock, reminding us of Diamond Dave's many similarities to Jim Dandy from Black Oak Arkansas. This is another one that goes back to 1974, evidenced by its inclusion on the 1974 Cherokee Studios demo, along with "Take Your Whiskey Home," both in 1980 quite faithful to the originals. Outside of the bluegrass lark, this one's the closest thing to the melodic Van Halen rock of "Little Dreamer," "Feel Your Love Tonight," and "Beautiful Girls" on the record. One intriguing wrinkle: The song ends and then the building blocks of a new song start, informally known as "Growth." Apparently, this was to open the following record, but it was not to be, which is no loss, given that it's kinda unremarkable.

No surprise, but Women and Children First went platinum within a couple months of issue, en route to its current triple-platinum status, albeit with the last attempts by management at certification now going back thirty years. As for the Billboard charts, the album peaked at #6, ensuring that this band of increasingly badder bad boys could continue to wreak havoc at least for another year, armed with a record that admirably ceded no ground to conventional commerciality.

The wardrobe department gets a little nutty, 1980.

10
WHY CAN'T THIS BE LOVE

EDDIE MARRIES VALERIE BERTINELLI

Valerie Bertinelli was two weeks shy of 21 years old and Eddie but 26 when the two young stars tied the knot on April 11, 1981. Eddie and the *One Day at a Time* TV actress had met at a Van Halen tour date on August 29, 1980, in Valerie's hometown of Shreveport, Louisiana, with Valerie using her showbiz connections to get backstage. She remembers first becoming enamored with Eddie after seeing his picture on the cover of her brother's copy of *Women and Children First*. Once together, they became a bit of a glamour couple, notable for looking like doppelgängers of each other: same hair, same eyes, same smile. Valerie had always defended the union as less of a mismatch than people thought. Meeting in the middle, she intimated that (a) Eddie was shy and reserved and sweet in his private life, less of a wild man than reported, and (b) she wasn't exactly the perfect angel that her cultivated TV image would suggest.

The two were married at St. Paul's Catholic Church in Westwood, California, but all did not go well. As manager Noel Monk relates, things were fine at the wedding, but leading up to the reception, Valerie had to deal with Eddie throwing up in the toilet after his heavy boozing before the swanky affair. After briefly considering canceling, she got Eddie together enough to go through with it.

This would represent a recurring theme throughout the couple's long but sometimes rocky marriage, with Valerie pained by Eddie's boozing and cocaine use. To add to the drama, even before the wedding, Eddie would be slapped with a paternity suit, which fortunately ended in his favor after he took a blood test that was to come out negative. In later years, when drug and alcohol abuse continued, Valerie was additionally angry at Eddie for not kicking smoking despite being diagnosed with oral cancer.

The couple's marriage would end first in separation and then an amicable divorce—without lawyers, only a mediator—on December 20, 2007. Capping off a union of more than twenty years, the two remained civil with each other and lived nearby. They even attended each other's second weddings, with Valerie befriending Eddie's second wife Janie Liszewski, and the two of them, along with Eddie and Valerie's son Wolfgang, being together when Eddie passed on. In fact, Alex Van Halen, an ordained minister, officiated not only Eddie's marriage to Janie in 2009 but also Valerie's marriage to financial planner Tom Vitale two years later.

By the time of their new unions, Valerie and Eddie had made amends, expressing their love for each other and the admission that both of them had contributed to their marriage's dissolution. In the end, Valerie's second marriage was over after ten years, and as Valerie explains in her book, it seems that at the time of Eddie's death, Janie and Eddie had been separated for a number of years as well. Valerie has since reflected that given the strong bond she and Eddie had maintained, had Eddie beaten cancer, perhaps the two of them might have rekindled their romance.

Eddie Van Halen and Valerie Bertinelli at their wedding at St. Paul's Catholic Church in Westwood, California, April 11, 1981

11
UNCHAINED
IT'S EDDIE'S ALBUM, FAIR WARNING

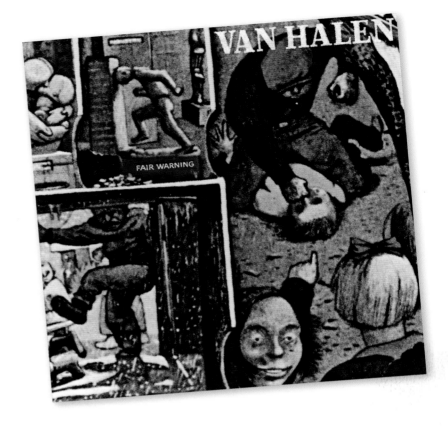

Like AC/DC's *Back in Black*, collective consciousness of *Fair Warning*, issued April 29, 1981, is sent darker by its album cover, although in Van Halen's case, it's also because none of the happy-slappy songs became hits. As we'd find out, the making of the record—same team, same place—was fraught with tensions, particularly between Dave and Eddie. Let's put it simply because it's the right word—Dave was jealous of Eddie's shiny new marriage to Valerie, and he was also jealous of Eddie being constantly praised for his guitar prowess.

At the music end, Eddie saw in the band, and in Ted Templeman, people who wanted to keep it fast and loose, while the maestro wanted to spend a little more time on this fourth album. His solution was to collar engineer Donn Landee and take him into the studio in the wee hours after everyone had packed up and redo his solos and add extra overdubs. To his annoyance, he says nobody seemed to notice. A year down the line and after the next album, he would remark that *Fair Warning* was his favorite Van Halen record in terms of guitar solos. Also different was that Eddie went into the studio with basic ideas and not-finished songs, let alone songs worked out live in the clubs. As he puts it, the songs were essentially built in the studio.

The end result was an album that indeed felt a little more finished, although it was no longer and larger than any of the band's previous low-value propositions. Nor was the product mix much different. As I say, it's my belief this narrative of melancholy or somberness around the record comes from the grainy and grim cover art (a detail of a William Kurelek painting), the fact that "So This Is Love?" stiffed as a single, and indeed the fact that two of the four most ornery songs on the album, "Mean Street" and "Unchained," became massive classic rock radio staples and even bigger fan favorites, usually making the top five or ten on any given poll.

It's "Mean Street" that opens the album, and immediately we can hear that the presentation is less ragged than on *Women and Children First*. The song is a heavy metal tour de force, with muscular drums gorgeously recorded and parts welded together firmly across five minutes of action. Next comes ""Dirty Movies"" (yes, with its own set of double quotes), and the band maintains its heaviness, only this time with a funkier groove. Eddie demonstrates a rare use of slide, and Alex, for the second song in a row, is double fisted on the high-hat. "Sinner's Swing!" (working title "Get Out and Push") is built on a speedy stop/start structure like "Romeo Delight" from the last album, although in the spaces, Alex maintains the beat with snare whacks. "Hear About It Later" is smeary pop metal like "Feel Your Love Tonight." Still, it's full band and acceptably serious, with lush backing vocals like every song so far. It closes a first side that is all business, four solid songs, nothing extraneous, seventeen minutes like regular people.

Side 2 opens just as strong with "Unchained" (working title "Hit the Ground Running"), featuring Eddie utilizing drop-D tuning and a distinctive flanger effect on the intro and chorus riff. There's also a thoughtful switching up of the time on the pre-chorus, all told, making for a smart construct for this happy headbanger of a track.

But like the last record, it's almost like as the night wears on, the band runs out of juice. "Push Comes to Shove" is drunk disco, missing the mark on an intended tribute to reggae, and "So This Is Love?"—working title "Flesh and Blood (Banana Oil)"—is slightly drunk, jammy, shuffling R&B. Then there's a two-minute instrumental that sounds like yer brain melting at 3 a.m.—anything but a "Sunday Afternoon in the Park." This is followed by an experimental metal number, also but two minutes long. Not only is it cool that Eddie, with

Above and opposite: Cobo
Hall, Detroit, July 3, 1981

a synthesizer riff, invents industrial metal, but "One Foot Out the Door" also delivers this writer's favorite Alex fill ever, heard just before the one-minute mark. As well, the whole back half features Eddie wailing away. At the fade, he hits these slashing, rhythmic, and somehow triumphant chords that serve as the perfect finale to this high-impact extended solo. In essence, this closing passage serves as a metaphor for the fact that *Fair Warning* would be framed as the record upon which Eddie took the highest degree of ownership. It took the longest thus far, it was the most expensive, and Eddie talked about how he lost a lot of sleep during its construction, as well as a lot of weight, saying that he was down to 125 pounds due to the stress of his around-the-clock care.

Fair Warning turned out to be the sales lagger of the Diamond Dave era, going platinum four months after release but then topping out at double-platinum. Still, with "Mean Street" and "Unchained" doing so much of the heavy lifting, it's well regarded by many of the more dedicated, studious Van Halen fans as sort of the third of a trilogy of records that comprise the obscurant, creatively reckless heart of the Van Halen experience and, conversely, the fourth and last of the classics.

Alex and a four-bass drum kit, Detroit, 1981

The wardrobe department strikes again, Detroit, 1981.

12
PUSH COMES TO SHOVE

THE CONTENTIOUS FIFTH ALBUM, DIVER DOWN

Completing the tour cycle for *Fair Warning* without a hit single, Van Halen were dealing with pressure from the label—as well as Ted Templeman and David Lee Roth—to deliver, with this faction in agreement that some choice covers might do the trick. *Diver Down*, issued April 14, 1982, would find the band relenting significantly, much to the disdain of Eddie, who had been mildly blamed for the relative failure of the previous year's record.

Most contentious would be "Dancing in the Street," which Eddie hated and yet did his best creative work on, turning in a burbling echo guitar and Minimoog riff that transformed the Martha Reeves and the Vandellas classic—it hit #38 on the Billboard charts. Then there was the opening track "Where Have All the Good Times Gone!" by The Kinks, which got to an impressive #17. Finally, the band worked up a happy-time rendition of Roy Orbison's "(Oh) Pretty Woman," complete with celebrated video, which shot to #12. All told, it must be said that this other approach worked, with *Diver Down* selling briskly en route to its current status at a tidy four-times-platinum.

But Van Halen weren't done with the covers. "Big Bad Bill (Is Sweet William Now)" featured family patriarch Jan Van Halen on clarinet, and "Happy Trails" was sung a cappella. If this suite of five questionable song choices wasn't enough, there were also three named instrumentals of little consequence.

This left "room" for only four conventional Van Halen tracks, and even "Secrets," a sort of jazzy shuffle, would have been called some sort of novelty outlier if it had been on one of the previous albums. "Hang 'em High" is a fast and loose rocker that plays third fiddle to "Sinner's Swing!" and "Romeo Delight," notably dragged down by Dave's conversational vocal, not that the riff bears much quality either. Next there's "The Full Bug," a clunky shuffle, and we're looking at fully three originals that seem half-baked and under-written, with phoned-in performances not much more inspiring than "Where Have All the Good Times Gone!," which sounds like a demo. Finally, there's "Little Guitars," which, although also poppy and perky, is a bit of an unheralded classic. It's named that because Eddie played it on a miniature Les Paul. Its intro, played on a nylon string acoustic, sets the tone for a sort of zesty Tex-Mex experience, hence Dave beginning his lyric with "Senorita."

Much to the annoyance of many Van Halen fans, their mainstream experience across the summery *Hide Your Sheep* tour cycle would amount to hearing "(Oh) Pretty Woman" and "Dancing in the Street" all over radio. There was a sense that their heroes had given up on art and heavy metal and had become a jukebox. No one else was complaining, though, with the album peaking at #3 on the Billboard charts and hanging around for an astounding sixty-five weeks. And even the most curmudgeonly of fans couldn't deny that *Diver Down* was a relentlessly cheerful experience—as the ad for it proclaimed, "*Diver Down*, Temperature Up."

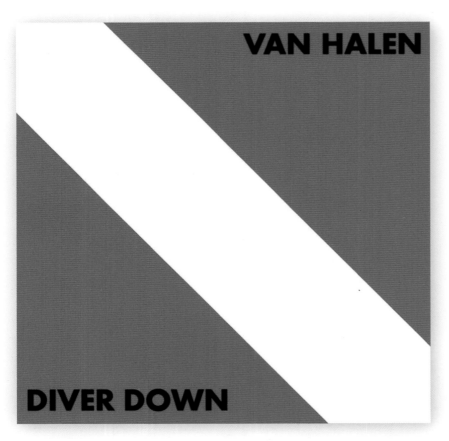

VAN HALEN

DIVER DOWN

Double the fun on the *Diver Down* campaign, Madison Square Garden, New York City, October 8, 1982. Support on the night came from After the Fire.

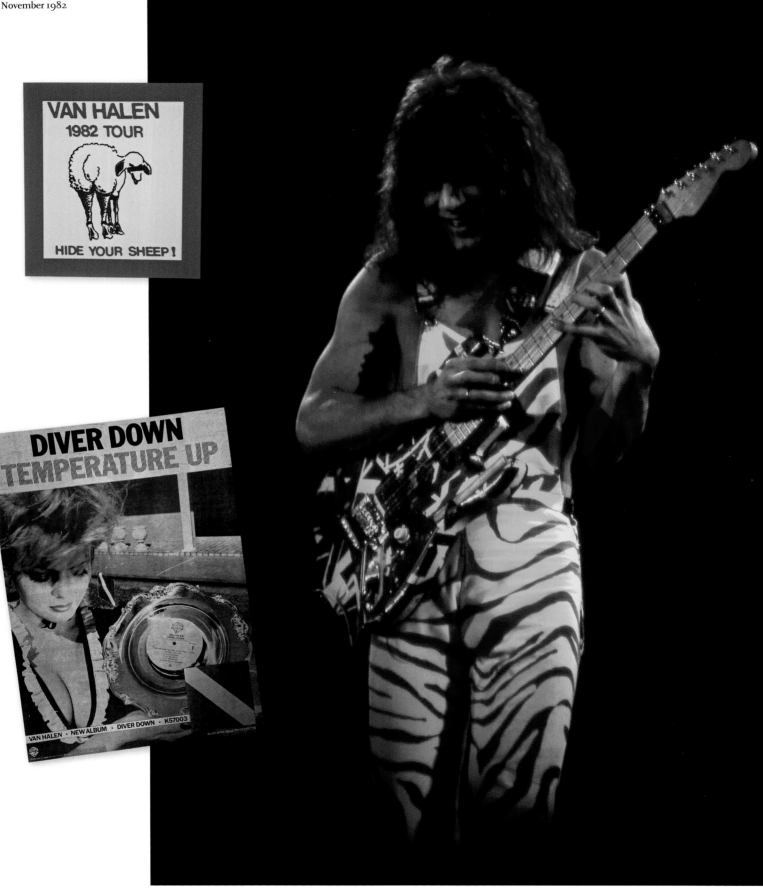

King Edward,
November 1982

VAN HALEN
1982 TOUR

HIDE YOUR SHEEP!

DIVER DOWN
TEMPERATURE UP

VAN HALEN · NEW ALBUM · DIVER DOWN · K57003

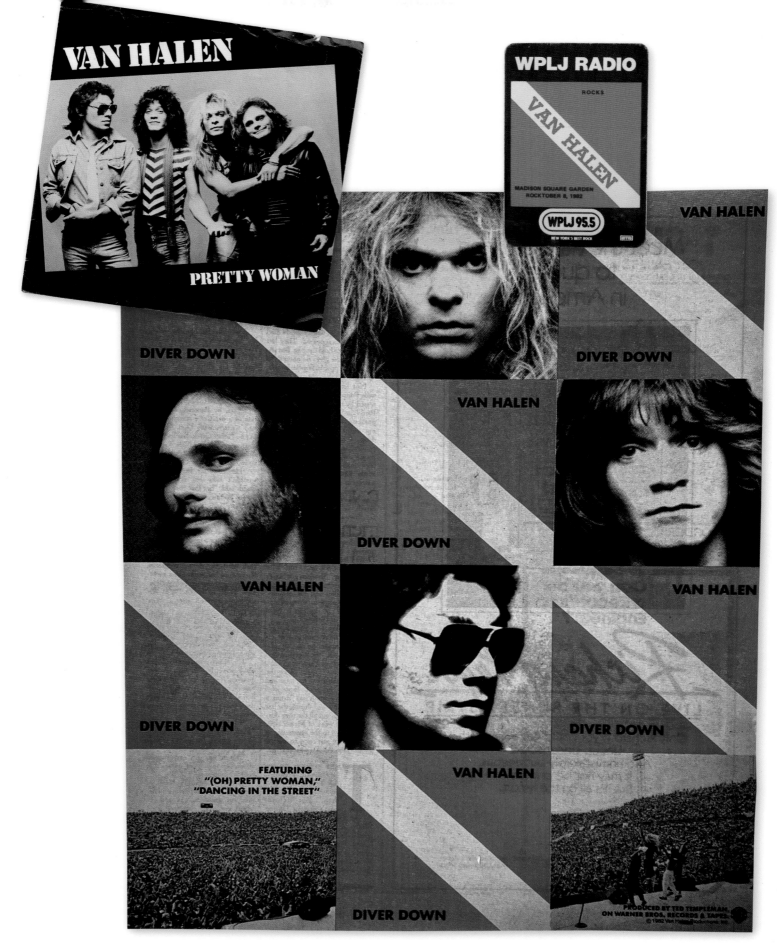

13

LITTLE GUITARS

EDDIE PLAYS ON MICHAEL JACKSON'S THRILLER

Eddie thought it was a prank call when producer Quincy Jones phoned him up to request that he stick a guitar solo on a Michael Jackson song. According to Jones, it took four calls before he could gain Eddie's trust. With respect to "Beat It," Jones and Jackson had the idea to make a rock song, but one that kids might like, even if the lyric was a denouncement of gang violence, inspired by Jackson's childhood in Gary, Indiana. And the song indeed lives and breathes on an iconic guitar riff and a pumping, up-tempo rock beat, with Eddie's solo serving as an underscoring of the song's crossover mandate.

For his part, Eddie and the guys had a handshake agreement not to do anybody else's sessions. But he figured, who's going to find out? Jackson wasn't a massive star at this point. That would only happen *after* this new record—*Thriller*, issued November 29, 1982—went on to sell seventy million copies worldwide, making it the biggest blockbuster of all time. As well, Eddie has said that Dave was up the Amazon, Michael was at Disneyland, and Alex was in Canada, so there was nobody around to ask.

In the studio, Jackson had been in tears, having been working on voice-overs in the room next door for the audiobook version of *E.T.* and having just gone through an emotional scene. But he wasn't there when Eddie and Jones and the engineers got Eddie onto tape. Eddie meekly suggested that he'd like to change the chords underneath his part, given that there were no chord changes at all. What we hear is, in fact, a subtly inverted version of the verse chords, in a dependable "Louie Louie"–type pattern—in other words, nothing fancy, even if it follows a fairly dramatic introductory break passage. Eddie says that the engineer moved some pieces around and made it work in less than ten minutes and that he proceeded to do two versions, completing his parts in under half an hour, on a Hartley-Thompson amp borrowed from fusion great Allan Holdsworth.

Jackson, upon hearing the results, told Eddie, "I really like that high fast stuff you do." He was also appreciative of the fact that Eddie took the effort to make a minor change to the song, in the interest of making it better. His solo lasts a little less than thirty seconds and is actually both atonal and restrained by Van Halen standards, and also comparatively clean, not very metal. Truth be told, it's kind of clunky.

In the end, Eddie did his part on the house as a favor to Jones. All he had requested was a case of beer and a promise that Jackson would teach him how to dance. He didn't regret not asking for "points" on the record, despite howls of derision from management and his bandmates after the album had blown up. Ultimately, he couldn't keep his own secret about the cameo. Scanning the racks at the Tower Records in Sherman Oaks one day, "Beat It" was playing when he overheard a couple of guys sneering at this guitarist trying to copy Eddie. He tapped them on the shoulder and informed them, "That's me."

Eddie guests with the King of Pop at a stop on The Jacksons' *Victory* tour at Texas Stadium, July 14, 1984.

14
PLEASURE DOME
THE BIRTH OF 5150 STUDIOS

Left and opposite: Eddie and Alex at 5150 studio in 1993. Working at home thirty years before it became "a thing."

It was the bad experience of getting steamrolled by *Diver Down* that resulted in Donn Landee and Eddie building home studio 5150, the mad lab that allowed the maestro to head down the rabbit hole and become the greatest plucker and strummer since Jimi Hendrix and, with the passage of the years, arguably the greatest of all time. Additionally, as Eddie told MTV's Chris Connelly on a tour of the place in 1998, he didn't want to wind up as "the world's biggest cover band, so to speak." The studio meant that Eddie would get his hurricane of ideas on tape and catalogued. By being able to work conveniently at home and at all hours, (a) he'd never experience a paucity of music and (b) he'd be in significant control of the recording process, evidenced by the fact that virtually all the Van Halen music moving forward would be recorded at 5150.

Construction began in 1983 at Eddie's 3371 Coldwater Canyon home in Studio City and then periodically picked up again throughout the months and years. To get around zoning laws, Eddie told the municipal inspector that he was building a racquetball court. Explaining the excessive "two-foot-thick cinderblock and rebar-enforced concrete fill" walls, Eddie, ever thoughtful of his neighbors, said that he liked to play late at night and hits the ball really hard.

The *For Unlawful Carnal Knowledge* sessions resulted in another small room, and the *III* album required knocking down a wall to expand that room. Yet, as Eddie explains, he wrote the *III* album in his bathroom studio, which was equipped with the same board he had in the main room.

Besides the crucial role of the studio in the construction of Van Halen albums, it also provided a means for Eddie to record all of his many hundreds of hours of ideas. Eventually he had amassed a massive tape library and had a method of accounting for what was there, but his "Radio Shack" computer's hard drive crashed and proved unrecoverable. The documenting process was never repeated because, as Eddie puts it, "the only person that can do that is me, because nobody knows what I like." 5150 would also serve as the lab where Eddie and his studio engineer and manager George Saer (starting in '98) would go wild with electronics, building all manner of gear an' gizmo, eventually resulting in a vibrant side hustle in Eddie-branded guitars and effects.

The workspace was never glamorous. It began as a cramped six-hundred-foot room that had to be wrapped in grounded chicken-wire fencing to negate the signal coming in from the powerful sports radio station nearby. The expansion for the 1991 album resulted in a doubling of size, a new mixing board, and a drum room for Alex. There was also a makeshift arcade area. In 1999, Eddie added a new mixing desk and a Mellotron, although we'd only ever get one more Van Halen album, and there's no Mellotron on it.

To this day, the studio is still in use, with Eddie's son Wolfgang using it in the creation of music for his Mammoth WVH project. The mystery of what's on the tapes—and what to do with them— remains unsolved, with Wolfgang reluctant to go there, still mourning his father's passing.

15
LIGHT UP THE SKY

VAN HALEN HEADLINE THE US FESTIVAL

Victory or victory lap? That's the lingering narrative to fall out of Van Halen's historic headline stand at Steve Wozniak's immense four-day US Festival, dropping like an atomic bomb onto Glen Helen Regional Park in San Bernardino, California, May 28 to June 4, 1983.

It was a victory in a number of ways. First, bestowed upon Van Halen was the widely publicized world record for the largest payday for a single concert of all time, at $1.5 million (even if Van Halen had to spend half a million to get their gear there and execute). Second, this was a celebration of Van Halen at their apex. They'd completed the wildly successful *Diver Down* tour, culminating in their first visit to South America, finishing up in mid-February. Eddie was already making use of his new home studio, constructing what would become *1984*. Most exciting tour ever, partway through the band's biggest triumph on record . . . yes, although it's an abstraction, parachute into it the band's most famous concert appearance ever, and this is the absolute zenith of zesty living in the life cycle of Van Halen.

Third, Van Halen wound up representing, by proxy, a victory for all of heavy metal. The first day of the festival, May 28, was coined "New Wave Day," and barely remembered are headliners The Clash, out of their element and environment in every possible way. May 30, now known as "Rock Day," featured another pile of bands, of which only David Bowie's performance is ever really reminisced over. Up into June 4, there was a "Country Day," which is completely forgotten. But May 29 was "Heavy Metal Day," and it took all the glory, attracting the biggest crowd, with Van Halen headlining over Quiet Riot, Mötley Crüe, Ozzy Osbourne, Judas Priest, Triumph, and Scorpions. As well, it should not go unnoticed that the two baby bands on the bill were mini-me versions of the showy show closers.

But in what way was Van Halen at the US Festival as much a victory lap as it was a victory? Well, the band's actual performance is as much notorious as it is lauded. Interviewing with MTV backstage long before stage time, it was obvious that Dave was already drunk. By the time the band hits the stage, he had become as much a dangerous loose wheel as an explosive but jocular loose cannon, rambling, establishing a casual relationship with the lyrics, and generally making a case for why hair metal, new this year, would one day have to die. Put another way, he was less so gunning hard for the Formula One finish line but more like hanging out of the car, pumping his fist, shouting and pointing, waving the flag, and weaving.

As the years add up, this narrative has been ossifying. Perhaps the band's less-than-perfect US Festival stand represents the cresting of the Van Wailin' roller-coaster car before descent. To be sure, there is a blindingly successful album and tour to come. But maybe, just, maybe, as the lights went down on the dusty sunburned throngs at the US Festival—Van Halen closing the show with two covers, "You Really Got Me" and an embedded "Happy Trails"—we might have just witnessed as good as it was ever going to get between Eddie and Alex on one side, and Dave and, to a lesser extent, Michael on the other.

Despite the boozing, Dave managed to do *this* at the band's historic ramble of a gig at the US Festival, May 29, 1983.

16

ATOMIC PUNK

VAN HALEN SCORE MASSIVE
HIT WITH 1984

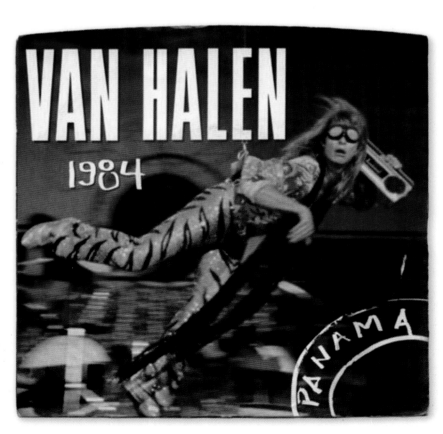

Salient in the title, *1984* reminds us that after five years with an album every year, Van Halen had finally skipped one. And it wasn't that 1983 was stuffed with concerts either, containing just the fairly robust South American tour plus the US Festival stand. Instead, Eddie worked five times as hard and everybody else twice as hard on a record that would become a milestone, *1984*, issued January 9, just into the new year.

Inspired by jamming in Frank Zappa's basement studio, Eddie built his own, which turned out to be an ingenious way of wresting the controls back from Ted Templeman, as well as away from the prying eyes of Dave and the label. As he did with *Fair Warning*, Eddie collaborated more so with Donn Landee on the building of the studio and then the music for the new album, with Templeman being less at home here on Eddie's turf. As a result, there'd be no covers nonsense to the new album, and Eddie would also win the war with Dave and Templeman over the inclusion of keyboard-heavy tracks "I'll Wait" and "Jump," the latter of which had been debated at this point for a couple of years.

Meanwhile, as the music was being layered and leveled up by Eddie and Landee, Dave would be driven around Los Angeles in an orange and white '51 Mercury convertible by his roadie Larry Hostler, running the music over and over and writing lyrics, periodically bouncing ideas off of his chauffeur and muse.

The end result would be an album with conversation pieces everywhere. As an opener, evocative of the record before, "1984" is a short instrumental piece, featuring Eddie playing around with his new Oberheim OB-8 while he watched his studio get built. Then we're into the shocking "Jump," issued as an advance single but now taking pride and place as the first real song on the album. It's of course living and dying on a stark and simple keyboard riff, but there's a darkness, too: Dave says the lyric was inspired by watching someone on the verge of committing suicide by jumping off a building.

Next comes the third single, "Panama," written about a car called that and inspired, according to Eddie, by the simple chordage of AC/DC. "Top Jimmy" is a quick and nimble guitar showcase dedicated to James Paul Koncek, the front man of a local R&B band called Top Jimmy & the Rhythm Pigs. Closing side 1 is "Drop Dead Legs," a slow and funky hard rocker reminiscent of "Beautiful Girls" as well as Aerosmith in that sort of "Last Child" zone.

Over to side 2 we have the album's fourth and final single, "Hot for Teacher," the next in the line of about a half-dozen "OTT" Van Halen songs, this time with deft double-bass drum work from Alex, most prominent on the novel beginning, essentially a drum solo. There's not much to the riff here, with Eddie playing a sort of pinched rhythm guitar (see also "Top Jimmy"), allowing Alex to thunder away while Dave delivers his update on Alice Cooper's "School's Out," only this time it's "school's in."

"I'll Wait," cowritten by Templeman's buddy Michael McDonald from The Doobie Brothers, was issued as the album's second single. Any dissent over including the songs on *1984* seems to be drowned out by Alex's powerfully and crisply recorded drums, which add crucial excitement, given the thinnest of premises up top.

First night of the 1984
tour campaign at the
Coliseum in Jacksonville,
Florida, January 18, 1984.
Supporting on the first leg
was Autograph.

Next we get action-packed heavy metal rocker "Girl Gone Bad," which has roots back to the live, jammed version of "Somebody Get Me a Doctor." Eddie tells the story of how the idea for the music came to him at an inopportune time: It was the middle of the night, and he and Valerie were in a rented hotel room, with Eddie sneaking away into a closet to work on the song so as not to waken his wife. *1984* closes with an even heavier number, with "House of Pain" going back to the band's club days, representing the most adjacent conceptual posture to 2012's *A Different Kind of Truth*. In other words, it's the last of a string of these and even more so feels like it could fit on that final Van Halen album, dated and a bit rote compared with the rest of *1984*, although one supposes it's got more going for it than the "barely written" "Hot for Teacher" and "Panama." In fact, the music making at the verse is quite wacky, almost progressive rock, and then at the end, we're treated to a surprise jam that is practically an entirely new song idea.

Fueled by three of the most iconic videos in MTV history, *1984* flew up the charts, reaching #2 on the Billboard grid and #1 in Canada. As for the singles, "Hot for Teacher" hit #56, both "I'll Wait" and "Panama" got to #13, and "Jump" got all the way to #1. The quartet of tracks served as a half-album metaphor for the totality of the record and its shaking and baking. Two of the songs—the only two like this on the whole album—found Eddie exploring the modern synthesizer technology of the day, while the other two rocked harder than anything from *Diver Down*. And like I say, nor were there any covers or—it must be noted—any jokey nonrock songs of any sort. This was Van Halen big and all business, world beating at a level they'd never risen to since the debut, and all of it accomplishing while working from home.

Go ahead and jump, Madison Square Garden, New York City, March 30, 1984

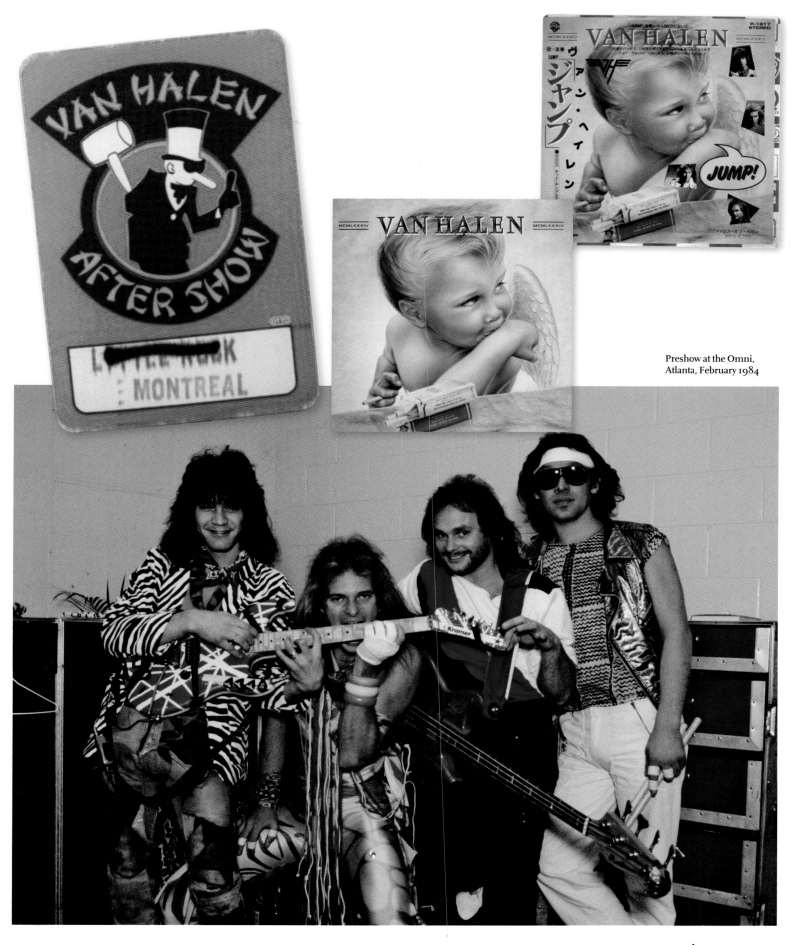

Preshow at the Omni,
Atlanta, February 1984

EAR CANDY ON VAN HALEN RECORDS

Nicolette Larson has the honor of providing the only female vocal on a Van Halen track with her work on "Could This Be Magic?."

The abused piano on "Strung Out" belonged to noted composer Marvin Hamlisch, whose house Eddie and Valerie were renting.

Steve Lukather, performing with Toto at Ahoy, The Netherlands, October 3, 1992. Luke provided backing vocals on "Top of the World" and "Never Enough."

Up to the band's fourth album, "Unchained" features a lingering mellow respite where Dave riffs like Frank Zappa. Then we hear Templeman over the studio intercom going, "Come on, Dave, give me a break," to which Dave answers, "Heh hey hey, one break, coming up!" But he's wrong. That kinda was the break, and what follows is just another round of the chorus. On the next song, "Dirty Movies," it sounds like the band members are hanging out at the strip club.

Next comes *Diver Down*, where on "Cathedral," Eddie redefines playing the guitar by playing the volume knob of the guitar. There's also "Big Bad Bill (Is Sweet William Now)," on which Eddie's and Alex's father Jan plays the clarinet. On "Intruder," Eddie rubs a can of Schlitz Malt Liquor against his strings and Dave is credited with synthesizers. Even if as ear candy, neither effect is that sweet. Plus, there's cowbell on "Dancing in the Street," harmonica on "The Full Bug," and the jokey and a cappella "Happy Trails," at 1:06, is essentially an entire song presented in the spirit of ear candy.

From the smash hit *1984* album, "Panama" features throaty revs from Eddie's own 1972 Lamborghini Miura S, backed up to the studio door and miked at the tailpipe. "Hot for Teacher" re-creates the sound of a high school classroom, although I don't recall ever seeing or hearing a beer bottle skitter across the floor. With Dave playing the wiseacre, these sound picture "verses" to the song bring back memories of Cheech and Chong's "Sister Mary Elephant" sketch from 1972.

Traversing into the Sammy Hagar years, "Poundcake" famously features Eddie running a power drill over his guitar strings, evoking images of Jackyl's Jesse James Dupree and his chainsaw. But even before that happens, very quietly, Alex says, "Ain't that some shit?" Eddie says, "Okay, ready to go?" Then it's, "Yeah," "Yeah?," "Let's do it," and "All right." Moving to the end of the same album, Toto's Steve Lukather provides backing vocals to "Top of the World," as he does on the next record's "Never Enough."

And speaking of *Balance*, the chanting at the beginning of "The Seventh Seal" is courtesy of The Monks of Gyuto Tantric University. "Strung Out" features Eddie abusing a white grand piano by dropping batteries, cutlery, and ping-pong balls on the strings. Eddie and Valerie had rented a house from noted composer Marvin Hamlisch in the early 1980s, and this piano was his. Eddie reportedly had broken a few strings in the process of putting together this minute-and-a-half sound collage. Speaking of Valerie, "Baluchitherium" was titled by her, using the name assigned to the largest land mammal ever to walk the earth. At the end, you can hear Sherman, the couple's dalmatian, barking. To entice him to the mic, they attached a hot dog wiener to it, and then to get him to bark, they played a sample of a fire engine siren. The other animal sounds (insects, elephants) are generated by Eddie on guitar. You can also hear dogs barking on *III*'s "As Is" and on *A Different Kind of Truth*'s "Honeybabysweetiedoll."

Wrapping up, our tour concludes with wind chimes on "Deja Vu," Eddie dragging a stick along the pavement on "Dirty Water Dog," and best of all, "Big Fat Money," where we hear that distinct sound—rapidly panned back and forth—of a coin settling itself on a tabletop.

Van Halen always kept things interesting by adding amusing sounds to their records. This often took the form of effects added to conventional instruments, certainly guitars first, but also bass, drums, and keyboards (and not really vocals, come to think of it, although we've got Dave's CB radio voice on "Loss of Control," don't we?). But then there was pure ear candy, which tends to add interest and even commerciality, a formula exploited to great effect by The Beatles and Pink Floyd and, to a lesser extent, Led Zeppelin, Queen, and Aerosmith. In that light, put your headphones on and follow the bouncing ball.

The first sound we ever hear from the band is a dramatic drone on "Runnin' with the Devil," made by a series of horns from the band's own cars. They used it in the club days, but here we find Ted Templeman and Donn Landee getting serious with it. There's also a siren whistle at the end of the first guitar solo, at the 2:08 mark. Onto the next album, before the acoustic "Spanish Fly" short piece, there's a brief mumble from Eddie and a bit of rustling, as if we're sitting across the couch from him. Up to the end of the record, the last thing we hear is Dave planting a kiss.

Over to *Women and Children First*, "Could This Be Magic?" opens like a porch jam, and you can clearly hear that it's raining. When life gives you lemons . . . the band decided to leave the door open and stick a couple Neumann KM 84 mics out there, and the result is an authentic, scratchy sort of Led Zeppelin acoustic song. Also, we get the only female vocal ever on a Van Halen song, with Nicolette Larson providing significant backing vocals, although she's mixed a little distant. Larson was part of the Warner Bros. stable, and Templeman produced her first three albums. (She died in 1997.) Then there's "And the Cradle Will Rock . . ." where the opening torrent of sound, sensibly thought to be pick scrapes on a distorted guitar, was actually created by Eddie putting aggressively hit lower-register notes from a Wurlitzer electric piano through a flanger effect and a one-hundred-watt Marshall Plexi amp.

17
ONE FOOT OUT THE DOOR

THE ORIGINAL VAN HALEN PLAY THEIR FINAL SHOW

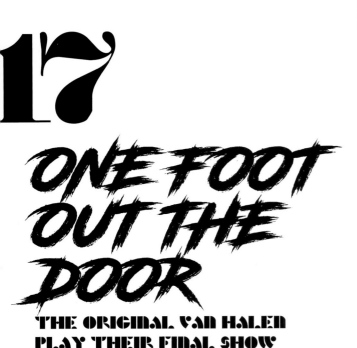

There are a few things unusual and even eerie about what would become the very last show ever of the classic Van Halen lineup. It took place September 2, 1984, at Zeppelinfield in Nuremberg, Germany, which for starters, was one of the prime Nazi party rally grounds, with the grandstand once featuring numerous swastika flags. Just the name Zeppelinfield has an air of finality to it.

It's also creepy that Van Halen had no idea this would be the end. Perched at the close of a mammoth tour in support of 1984 (the band's most rapidly embraced album, to be sure), the guys were miserable, with Dave traveling separately from the rest. Still, once they got back to the good ol' US of A, Dave spoke in interviews about jumping into the studio soon with the guys, while acknowledging but cracking jokes about the drama surrounding the band's fiery relations.

Also perhaps unsettling is that Van Halen were part of the massive Monsters of Rock package at this point, on this particular day playing to a crowd of forty-five thousand. They'd toured solid from January through July, ending triumphantly in Texas. But now with a month's break, they found themselves virtually as far away from home as they'd ever go, certainly spiritually, with Germany being nothing like Los Angeles, and performing as part of a pack, a Grand Central Station of metal makers. And they weren't even headlining. AC/DC closed the show, with Van Halen second to last, preceded by Ozzy Osbourne, and then down the card: Dio, Mötley Crüe, Y&T, Gary Moore, and local metal titans Accept.

Also, on the day, they were bathed in a sort of eerie, overcast light, with a big black-and-orange backdrop behind them and no help from typical nighttime concert lighting. As can be seen in footage of the band's performance of "Jump," Dave's prancing onstage calisthenic shtick was getting unbearable. His ego—he was even starting to brag about *that* in interviews—seemed to be celebrated with each gratuitous red unitard kick, and then accentuated with a twirl away from the camera, which every now and then leaned toward the feminine (not the effect he was looking for, I'm sure). At one point, over his onesie he's wearing American flag short shorts, and rather than thinking, "That looks cool," I'm now on the side of hollering, "You're desecrating the flag!" As for the rest of the guys, Alex has his electronic drums and Eddie's synthesizers are in full force, with Michael even going crazy with the pedals. But again, there's the palpable sense that Dave is utterly alone up there, blowing out the candles on his birthday cake and then retiring to his room to open his presents alone.

Set list-wise we get "Unchained," "Hot for Teacher," a drum solo, "On Fire," "Runnin' with the Devil," "Little Guitars," "House of Pain," a bass solo, "I'll Wait," "Everybody Wants Some!!," "(Oh) Pretty Woman," "1984," "Jump," a guitar solo, and then "Panama." Then, as we march toward the closing of a chapter, I may be letting my imagination run away with me, but I find the encore eerie as well. There's one lone song, and it's "You Really Got Me," the Kinks cover that got them signed in the first place, followed by "Happy Trails," which, like the historical significance of the concert and the very name of the venue, also drips with a sense of melancholy or at least reflective finality.

18

BOTTOMS UP!

"JUMP" WINS BEST STAGE PERFORMANCE AT FIRST MTV VIDEO MUSIC AWARDS

Smashing through to #1 on the charts was a bigger deal comparatively, but nonetheless, Van Halen also took home an award from the inaugural MTV Video Music Awards, held at the Radio City Music Hall in New York City on September 14, 1984. "Jump" won the Best Stage Performance prize, beating out David Bowie, Duran Duran, Bette Midler, and The Pretenders. Then again, Van Halen got beaten themselves elsewhere, losing out to Michael Jackson's "Thriller" for Best Overall Performance and to ZZ Top's "Legs" for Best Group Video.

Accepting the award from a discombobulated Ron Wood was Dave and Dave alone—and both of them were in red jackets. Dave said a few things about how American MTV was, how American Van Halen was, and how American Miss America was but got off the stage relatively unscathed, despite Wood mugging behind him all herky-jerky, clearly under the influence. Other big winners on the night included David Bowie, Cyndi Lauper, Eurythmics, The Police, ZZ Top, and Michael Jackson, with The Cars taking Video of the Year. Cleaning up, Herbie Hancock won five times for his innovative "Rockit" clip.

But yes, it was up to ZZ Top and Van Halen to support the hard rock side. ZZ Top had a clear narrative with their iconic *Eliminator* videos, but Van Halen were subtly building one as well, and that's the live performance thing. The "Jump" clip features the band throwing all manner of shape, much of it in hair metal slow motion. Dave's Mr. Show Biz the whole time, magically executing a couple of costume changes. Eddie, in a black-and-yellow tiger print jacket and patched jeans, grins, goofs, and twirls, pointing his Frankenstrat at the camera, with Michael selectively doing some of the same dance steps. Alex, in a green vest and powering his way around a massive kit, is captured close-up as well, with his drumming synched perfectly to the track, really driving home how rocking this song is at the bottom end.

The highlight of the video is also the highlight of the track, and that's the buoyant break section, which begins with Eddie soloing on guitar but then transitioning to angelic, almost '70s prog keyboards circa Styx. Alex and Michael keep the rhythm foundation exciting throughout, culminating in Alex's tom fill, which he punctuates with shimmering crash cymbal muted with his hand, uncommon in that there's no bass drum whack under it. All the while, director Peter Angelus makes sure to capture the key instrumental hooks as fast and furious as they come, even finding time to get a flash of martial arts from Dave.

Other than the keyboard solo, Eddie is filmed playing guitar, so there's a fair bit of incongruity given the prominent synth line. At one point, Dave helpfully plays an invisible keyboard, not helping. All told, "Jump" is a simple clip, but these guys aren't hams. They're the whole pig, as they say in the business. "Panama" was dealt more bells and whistles, and "Hot for Teacher" even had a plot. All three are heaps of fun, effervescently woven into the fabric of pop culture consciousness circa 1984, which ends up being the biggest year of Van Halen's career, toured rock-solid for seven months strapped to a rocket of a record also called *1984*.

Dave doing his best to blend in at the MTV Video Music Awards after-party at the Hard Rock Café in New York City

19

AIN'T TALKIN' BOUT LOVE

DIAMOND DAVE ISSUES *CRAZY FROM THE HEAT* ... THEN QUITS VAN HALEN

On January 28, 1985, David Lee Roth seized upon the worst of the myriad character traits Eddie and Alex couldn't stand about him and amplified them across a four-track EP called *Crazy from the Heat*. What's worse, although the majority of Van Halen fans recoiled in horror, witnessing in lurid technicolor videos for "Just a Gigolo/I Ain't Got Nobody" and "California Girls," many more must have bought the damn thing. *Crazy from the Heat* was gold by April and platinum in June. To add insult, Ted Templeman was producing and therefore picking sides.

At this point Dave was still part of Van Halen, although both camps' grasp on that version of reality was slipping fast. Upon the release in January of his fourteen-minute collection of show tunes, Dave openly reflected in conversation with Billboard that "from the first day" he'd always felt his days were numbered. The influential industry standard titled the article "Van Halen's Roth: Maybe It's Over."

March saw a summit between Eddie and Dave, where Dave expressed his desire to do a movie, also called *Crazy from the Heat*. Going on offense, he asked Eddie to score it, with the maestro declining politely but later letting fly how offended he was. For his part, Eddie talked about scaling down tour plans for the next album to a series of stadium shows, which Dave thought would shortchange the fans.

The following month saw an April Fools' Day joke from Dave saying that he'd quit Van Halen. Then there was the firing of longtime manager Noel Monk, with the band now rudderless, running things badly, and communicating even worse. Within the band, Alex had been the closest thing they had to a businessman, but he ran hot and was suspicious to a fault. Eddie, forget it.

Now taking shape, apparently, was some sort of agreement that the band take a year off. But then Dave's movie plans seem to have spoiled the idea of what a year off meant. There might have been suspicion of manipulation as well, with Eddie and Alex thinking Dave was already well along with his other plans before they talked. Besides, Dave was also antsy about a year away from rock 'n' roll, thinking he wanted a new band if that was the case. Back and forth it goes, with Alex then responding that it's Van Halen that are not going to wait for Dave to play movie star.

Meanwhile, the aforementioned over-the-top novelty songs are all over MTV, both being, again, all the cheesy Dave shuck-and-jive bits from the three *1984* videos renovated and exaggerated, with a backing track of easy listening by session musicians for soundtrack instead of Eddie, Michael, and Alex throwing down. On July 4, *Rolling Stone* reports that Van Halen is on "permanent hold," with Eddie stepping forward and telling America's top rock mag in mid-August that the band is over with. In other words, there's no talk of getting a new singer. Eddie is collaborating with Scandal vocalist Patty Smyth on some tunes, and he's got plans to do something with Pete Townshend as well. But what happens next would be something very different. As well, let's just say that, typical of what happens on the Boulevard of Broken Dreams, Diamond Dave would not become a movie star.

Act Two
THE RED ROCKER

2

Who needs 1984 when
you've got 1985?

20

SO THIS IS LOVE?

EDDIE JOINS SAMMY ONSTAGE AT FARM AID

The news that Sammy Hagar was going to join Van Halen snuck out gradually, with the resentments and recriminations beginning before the Farm Aid benefit and then emerging full-blown after the performance, with Bill "Electric" Church and Jesse Harms from Sammy's band most offended, along with Sammy's first wife Betsy, who warned him not to do it.

It all begins in Claudio Zampolli's auto shop. Eddie had his Lamborghini in for repairs and had told Zampolli that Dave had quit. Flash forward and Sammy has his black Ferrari 512, the star of the "I Can't Drive 55" video, in for a tune-up. Eddie walks in, sees the car, asks whose it is, and Zampolli tells him and suggests he get Sammy to join the band. Eddie calls him right from the shop, and a jam ensues that goes from noon to midnight, followed a few days later by a celebratory Mexican dinner out. Sammy hadn't been the only choice; Patty Smyth, Jimmy Barnes, and Eric Martin were also taken into consideration; but jamming with Sammy sealed the deal, with the guys even managing first baby steps toward a new record.

Flash forward to the inaugural Farm Aid, taking place on September 22, 1985, in Champaign, Illinois. Sammy and his band are at the height of their fame, performing a blazing set of three songs: "There's Only One Way to Rock, "Three Lock Box," and "I Can't Drive 55." Sammy's a ball of energy, running all over the stage, singing into his headset mic, and singing great. Soon it's time for Eddie and Sammy to play together in public for the first time. They do one song together, a brief but inspired version of Led Zeppelin's "Rock and Roll." The camaraderie is instant and palpable, and when Eddie finishes his action-packed

yet economical solo slot, Sammy just shakes his head in wonder. At the big windup, Eddie goes on and solos a bit on his own, with Sammy remarking, "The king, the king." As Sammy tells the story, this is where the national television coverage gets cut, ostensibly from the network getting madder and madder about how much Sammy is swearing. And here's where Sammy says he let it be known that he's joining Van Halen, but as he puts it, he "screws up" because it wasn't being broadcast.

Bassist Church says that he was fuming onstage and refused to "do the two-step" with Eddie when Eddie came over to try jam with him. He talks about seeing signs in the audience announcing the merger and even that what was happening in the crowd seemed suspiciously staged. Church wouldn't fly back on the private jet with the band, taking Amtrak instead. He didn't talk to Sammy again for months. Further irking Church, he says that neither Gary Pihl nor David Lauser could bring themselves to raise any objections.

In other words, in typical rock 'n' roller fashion, Sammy didn't exactly manage the communication of his career move all that directly or clearly. To be fair, perhaps there was half a mind that he could do both things at once, that there was no reason to end a thriving solo run that had finally paid off. And again, to make things worse, even the plan to put the news out nationwide on live TV had crashed like a Led Zeppelin. The career move itself was another matter: Manager Ed Leffler quickly worked out a deal to get Sammy extricated from his Geffen contract, and within weeks, The Red Rocker would be at 5150 making 5150.

Ed joins Sammy at Farm Aid, Champaign, Illinois, September 22, 1985. Sammy would return the favor and join Ed for many more performances after that.

21
MEAN STREET

EDDIE INDUCTED INTO HOLLYWOOD ROCKWALK

It's testimony to Eddie's impact that he was chosen to be among the very first class of inductees into the Hollywood RockWalk. The ceremony took place November 13, 1985, and kicked off the popular tourist attraction, situated in front of the Guitar Center at 7325 Sunset Boulevard in Los Angeles. In what has become a tradition, the elected musicians show up and place their hands in cement to create a print, in contrast to the Hollywood Walk of Fame, which is made from hand and footprints, too. There's a brass plaque and, in Eddie's case, a signature scrawled directly into the cement (later, the autographs would appear on smaller plaques). The complex has expanded since to include bronze busts and iconic rock star–used guitars in display cases.

King Edward was inducted along with Stevie Wonder and an impressive list of gear legends, including Robert Moog of Moog synthesizer fame; C. F. Martin III of Martin guitars; Remo Belli of Remo (known for drumheads); Jim Marshall, creator of the Marshall amp; Ted McCarty, creator of the Les Paul guitar; and Les Paul himself.

In attendance were Lita Ford, Bill Cosby's son Ennis, and Carlos Cavazo and Frankie Banali from Quiet Riot. Eddie's support team consisted of Michael Anthony, brother Alex, and wife Valerie. The absence of David Lee Roth could be for a myriad of reasons, but most pertinently, by this date he was out of the band. In fact, at the time of the ceremony, the guys had already been hard at work building what would become 5150.

It's nice that Cavazo was there, because he represented the next generation of this vibrant guitar hero consort that Eddie most significantly inspired. Putting aside the instrumental guitar hero cottage industry, featuring the likes of Joe Satriani, Vinnie Moore, Marty Friedman, Jason Becker, and Paul Gilbert, the new hair metal bands of the day each had their own Cavazo and Eddie, with the big ones being George Lynch, Jake E. Lee, Great White's Mark Kendall, and Warren DeMartini and Robbin Crosby from Ratt, soon to be joined by John Sykes, Slash, and Steve Vai, the latter of whom would release albums in both these categories influenced and inspired by Eddie.

And that's the point: Eddie is one of the key reasons competition in the axe department was so intense up and down the Sunset Strip, so it's fitting that the local hero would be feted at the inaugural RockWalk, living and creating close by, and celebrated in front of a place called Guitar Center. The tradition continues, with every RockWalk induction over the ensuing years making the news, its high standing bolstered by the fact that subsequent inductees are voted on by previous inductees, giving the institution a musician-centric disposition.

Artist Roberto Vargas speaks at the January 2021 unveiling of his Eddie Van Halen mural at the West Hollywood Guitar Center whose famous RockWalk honored Eddie in 1985.

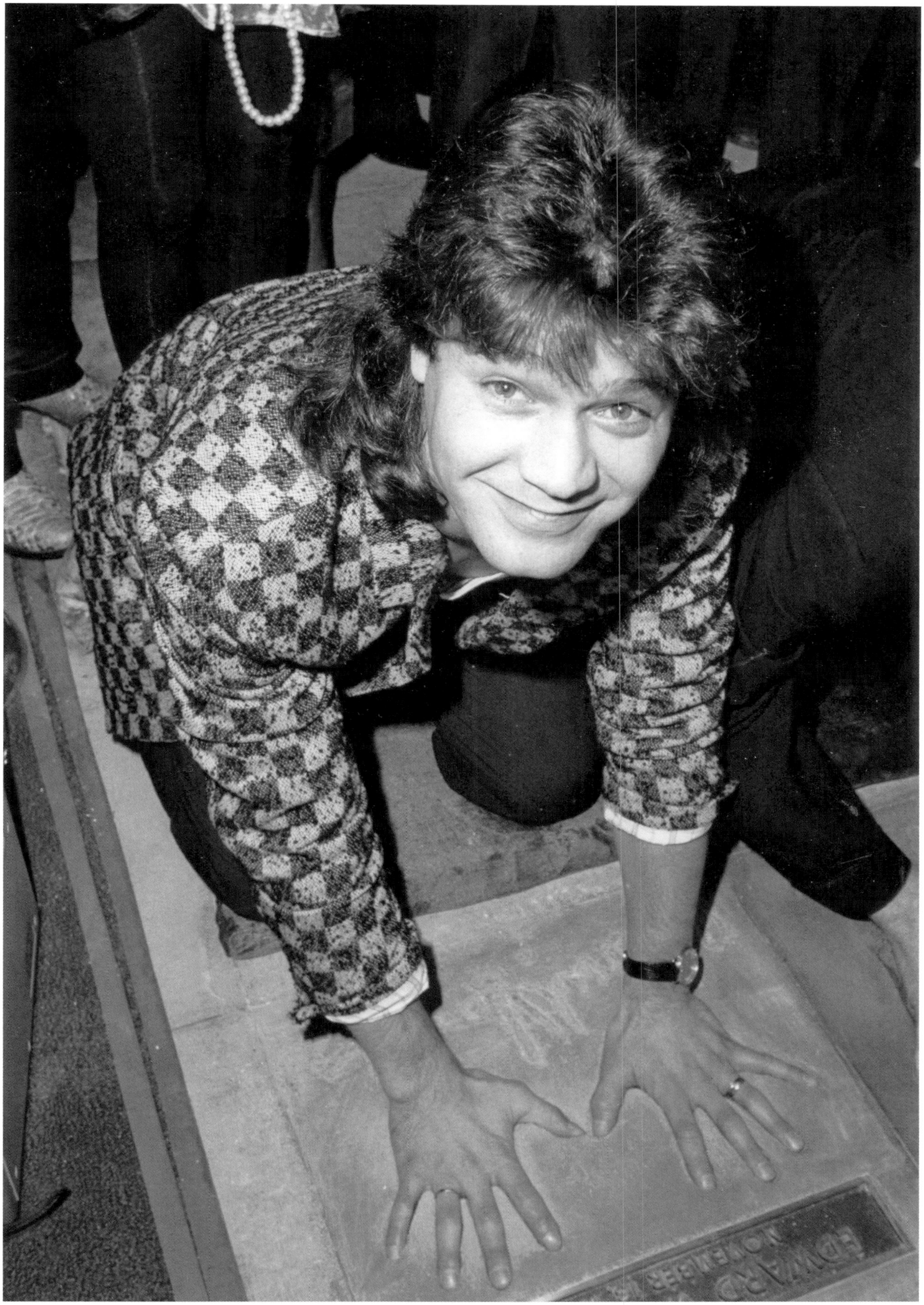

"I hope this comes off. I kinda need these." Outside Guitar Center on Sunset Boulevard, Hollywood, California, November 13, 1985

22

CABO WABO

SAMMY REPLACES DAVE FOR 5150

Alex shows Eddie how it's done. Backstage at Joe Louis Arena, Detroit, May 9, 1986

As Sammy fondly recalls any time he's asked about *5150*, work on the record was a breeze, blessed with inspiration upon jams and goodwill permeating the room. "Good Enough" and "Summer Nights" were first, with Sammy spontaneously riffing some tossed-off words atop rough chord structures. But then the guys hit upon "Why Can't This Be Love," propelled forward by Eddie enthusiastically playing keyboards through his guitar rig and Sammy filling in on guitar—this turned out to be a great utility function that had been missing with Dave.

Speaking of the exiled front man, Ted Templeman was now contracted with Dave, but they managed to retain Donn Landee, who did much of the heavy lifting, with Foreigner's Mick Jones in to provide an outside ear. The official production credit reads "Van Halen, Mick Jones and Donn Landee," which makes sense because mad scientist Eddie was pretty much a producer by this point, Sammy had been around the block a few times, and, after all, they were recording in Eddie's lab.

The band recorded from November of '85 through February of '86, with the album quickly to follow on March 24, 1986. Success at the cash registers was instant, and then the heated debate began about the contents. I've long maintained that *5150* represents a triumph of performance and production over songs. Others love the songs and dislike the production, while none deny the performance, a result of fortuitous chemistry among newlyweds.

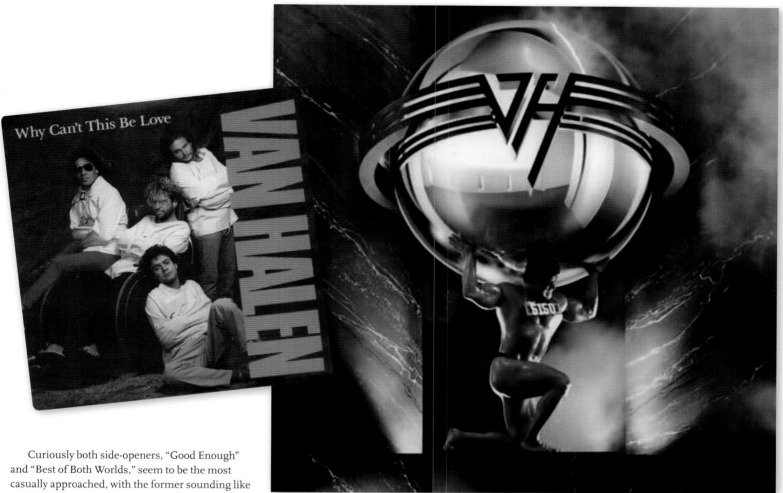

Curiously both side-openers, "Good Enough" and "Best of Both Worlds," seem to be the most casually approached, with the former sounding like a rewrite of the previously barely written "Panama" and the latter featuring some of the dullest riffing we'd ever hear from Eddie—predictable chords, played quiet and then played loud, kinda dull. But then again, "Best of Both Worlds" became a massive summery hit, serving as the sort of autobiographical celebration of the new situation, basically the merging of two large going concerns.

Also hugely successful were the two ballads, "Dreams" and "Love Walks In," each reaching #22 on the main Billboard chart. But "Dreams" was a ballad like "Jump" was a ballad, up-tempo, buoyed by the brightest of keyboards, while "Love Walks In" is much slower, a little dour, reminiscent of a couple of those smoky Foreigner smash hits. Again, Eddie is prominent on keys, his rig evolving and expanding. Of note as well, Landee had rectified the band's tendency in the Dave years to pan the guitars hard left, not that guitars are central to this album's being. Actually, what is more central is drum sound and drums, with Alex captured crisp and modern, with electronic bite applied to his snare and bass drums and most prevalently his toms. I've always maintained he's as much a part of the Van Halen "brown sound" as Eddie and that this record presents the most extreme example of this inclusive idea.

Elsewhere, "Get Up" delivers Van Halen's version of "extreme" heavy metal—this record's "Hot for Teacher," even if both those songs are undermined by a curious lack of quality at the guitar riff end of things, resulting in songs that are frantic and thin but more so with "Get Up," where we're sort of missing the bottom end. "Summer Nights," "'5150,'" and "Inside" form the lunch bucket core of the record, somewhat in the manner of the previous album's "Top Jimmy" and "Drop Dead Legs." This is where Eddie delivers the riffs, licks, and solos that make him the best example of a "shred"-level '80s guitarist but with loads of personality, accompanied by a band that is red-hot an' dazzled by the possibilities of where this could go.

That leaves the album's aforementioned masterpiece, "Why Can't This Be Love." If we can posit that Sammy brought a sort of John Mellencamp/heartland rock/Bryan Adams pop sensibility to the band, it's most creatively successful when they try harder and move beyond rote power ballads. "Dreams" is partway there, and "Why Can't This Be Love" takes it all the way toward pure glory. The chord changes at the verses are sophisticated, pondering, reflective, and the feel-good payoff with the chorus is massive. Millions agreed, sending the

song to #3 on the Billboard charts. "Why Can't This Be Love" achieves that hallowed Rubicon cross into the realm of anthemic, specifically at that clouds-parting chorus. But then again, also at the choruses, so do "Dreams," "Best of Both Worlds," and even deep track "Summer Nights."

The end result is an album fresh and summery like *Diver Down* and *1984* but altogether made brighter through Sammy's higher and more histrionic vocals and then, almost metaphorically, by the parallel brightness of the guitars, keyboards, and drums. I've lauded the performance and production, but there's also the panorama of the styles address and then the deft sequencing thereof, all across a respectable running time of forty-three minutes and not an instrumental interlude in sight. Overlaid onto this is the opulent art deco shimmer of the album cover and then, equally abstractly, arising out of the front-page-headline-making status of the vocalist change, the sense of hope and renewal shared by the band and its fans as they celebrated the summer of '86 together as one.

The new Van Halen performs on Halloween night, 1986, at the Cow Palace in San Francisco. It was the first of a four-night run supported by Bachman-Turner Overdrive, who had been out with the band since March.

23
DREAMS
5150 HITS #1 ON BILLBOARD ALBUM CHARTS

Nashville Municipal Auditorium, Nashville, April 20, 1986

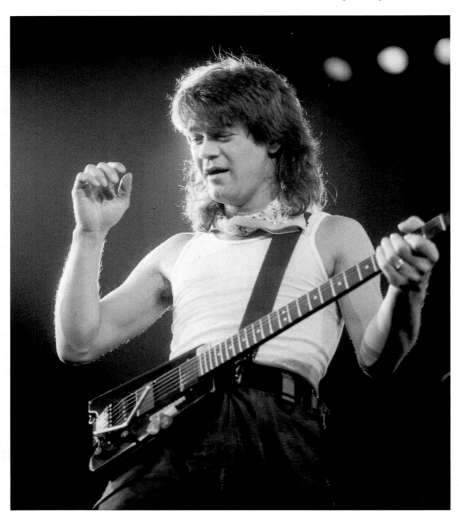

For the Red Rocker, it was the culmination of a career now thirteen years long, and all of it making records and nudging at that next level of acceptance. On April 25, 1986, exactly a month after its release date, 5150 would hit #1 on the Billboard charts, giving both Sammy as well as his three new band brothers their first chart-topping album ever, after which every album Sammy did with the band would also reach that pinnacle.

Not only that, buoyed by the effervescent "Why Can't This Be Love" as an initial single, and then put over the top by the equally warm and fuzzy "Dreams," the album would be certified gold, platinum, and double-platinum all at once a month later on May 28. And if you weren't cognizant of these statistics, Sammy made sure you heard about it from him, forevermore letting it be known the band never had a #1 with Dave (1984 was stopped at #2 by Thriller) and also claiming that 5150 was the fastest Warner Bros. album ever to go platinum, an assertion that can never be proven because it's complicated. In any event, blowing past double-platinum is the bigger accomplishment, with triple-platinum arriving soon enough as well, on October 10, 1986. 5150 currently sits at six-times-platinum, with the last attempt at certification being made back in 2004.

This proved once again that Van Halen—maybe even more so with Sammy as front man—was an inherently American experience. The U.S. results were the most impressive, with the album reaching #2 in Canada and selling triple-platinum at three hundred thousand copies. Australia and Germany proved decent enough, with the United Kingdom being a disappointment, giving the band a gold award for sixty thousand copies sold.

Still, back home the band could not be stopped, generating extra waves of excitement with the release of "Love Walks In" as a single in July of '86 and then "Best of Both Worlds" in October of that year. Looking around at the competition—and nobody is more competitive than Sammy—up and down the Sunset Strip,

Van Halen were #1 there as well. The biggest bands from the new guard couldn't match the box office Van Halen were generating. Closest were Ratt and Dokken, with Poison, Cinderella, and Guns N' Roses just getting going. As for the old guard, they were all hitting a wall. AC/DC, Scorpions, Kiss, Judas Priest, even the newer and shinier Iron Maiden and Ozzy and Ronnie James Dio as solo acts . . . they had all been having more fun a few years back, when Van Halen had a different front man. Moving ahead into 1987 and 1988, the aforementioned new glam metal bands would do brisk business, as would a surprising Aerosmith, but Van

Hagar would be right there with them, with none of the rest of the heritage acts particularly responding.

Bottom line, Van Halen "Mach II," as Sammy would call it, would roll right over the critics and criticism, through a subtle reinvention beyond just the change of front man, with sweeter, more presentable songs, brighter production values, and Eddie embracing the '80s through more prominent use of keyboards. It may not have been yer dad's Van Halen anymore, but that didn't seem to bother anybody back at the Warner Bros. offices.

The Meadowlands, East Rutherford, New Jersey, July 28, 1986

24

ICE CREAM MAN

DAVE ISSUES EAT 'EM AND SMILE

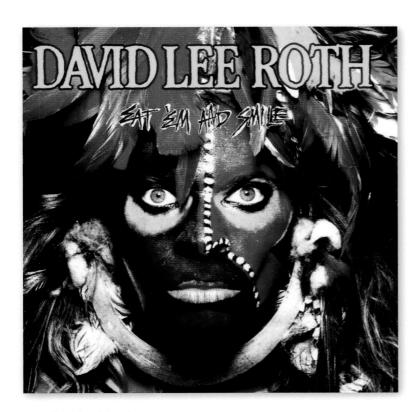

In what looked very much like a response to a shot across the bow, David Lee Roth emerged screaming and kicking a mere three months after the release of *5150* with a debut solo album called *Eat 'Em and Smile*. Issued July 7, 1986, the Ted Templeman–produced Warner Bros. album was prefaced by advance single "Yankee Rose," a suitable first peer into what Dave had in store for us.

What that turned out to be was a sort of lab-amped version of his old band. First turned up was Dave's own sartorial plumage, which he then foisted upon his hastily assembled band—namely, Steve Vai, Billy Sheehan, and Gregg Bissonette. And who were these guys anyway? Well, Vai was Eddie but not quite, Sheehan was Eddie but not quite, and Bissonette was Eddie but not quite, the last completed with a double bass flurry and flourish of Alex. The record they made together was *Diver Down* but not quite— frantic, casual, with three jokey covers and a couple of originals that were pretty jokey, too.

The lining up and knocking down of Van Halen tropes was pretty much overt, a statement in itself. "Shyboy," dredged from Sheehan's old Buffalo band Talas, and "Elephant Gun" were "Hot for Teacher" 2.0, or in current parlance, "Get Up" 2.0, while "Yankee Rose" was a look-in at the "Panama" riff. "Ladies Nite in Buffalo?," "Big Trouble," and "Bump and Grind" all had that funky hard rock feel found across many Van Halen songs, with Dave alternating comedy club zingers with life philosophy lessons that would look good on a bumper sticker, preferably on a convertible parked at the beach.

That leaves four songs, all of which turn the amps backward in the direction of *Crazy from the Heat*. Indeed all three of the covers, "Tobacco Road," "I'm Easy," and "That's Life," could have fit there fine, while original "Goin' Crazy!" reads like the title track from that record, now imagined as a full-length.

If we're to be kind, what Dave and Vai have built here (Vai was sort of musical director, because that's what entertainers have, right?) was a youthful, next-level Van Halen, where the players run circles around the originals like puppies around a big mama dog. And the lead singer? Well, same thing—this is Dave on a sugar and hormone high. I mean, while everybody else is pickin' and grinnin', Dave can barely contain his laughter while singing. *Skyscraper*, issued a year-and-a-half later, would be the same thing all over again, only this time Dave's support shredders would be huffing helium, while Dave, mountain climbing on the front cover, would be naturally higher on thinner air.

Eat 'Em and Smile would go platinum almost immediately (but not certify any further, burning out like fast food), while reaching #4 on the Billboard charts. Effervescent pop metal anthem "Goin' Crazy" would reach #66 on the singles chart, while conservative blues metal jam "Yankee Rose" would hit #16. At the time, Dave framed the album as some sort of soundtrack experience to his *Crazy from the Heat* movie, which never materialized. Instead, the band hit the road, dressed like Christmas trees, doing everything they could to make Van Hagar look old and slow.

25

"DIRTY MOVIES"
VAN HALEN ISSUES THE LIVE WITHOUT A NET CONCERT VIDEO

Veterans Memorial Coliseum, New Haven, Connecticut, August 1986

Van Halen with Sammy had been a smash hit as the band rolled into the New Haven Veterans Memorial Coliseum in New Haven, Connecticut, confident in putting $350,000 on the line in hopes of creating a concert video. The band filmed for two nights, August 26 and 27, but the first night yielded only some video footage, given that Eddie's wireless guitar kept cutting out. It was of no concern as the band rocked it hard the following night, thoroughly road tested by gigging continuously since the release of the 5150 album save for a break in June. Ergo, the final ninety-two-minute video required very little in the way of edits, other than moving a few songs around and deciding what not to include—namely, new songs "Good Enough" and "Dreams" as well as covers of "You Really Got Me," "Wild Thing," and the "Addicted to Love" excerpt the guys vamped in "Best of Both Worlds."

As for the official track list, the past is supported by four songs, or five if you count the closing cover of Led Zeppelin's "Rock and Roll," the fateful song that signaled a new Van Halen at Farm Aid. Dismissing their own past, partially in deference to Sammy, Van Halen played only "Panama" and "Ain't Talkin' 'bout Love" from the David Lee Roth era. Reinforcing the decision to hire Sammy, the band played two of the new guy's solo songs. Opener "There's Only One Way to Rock" was explosive, with Sammy and Eddie relentlessly dueling away on guitars. "I Can't Drive 55," however, wasn't so good here and was never great at extant concerts, given Alex's clunky four-on-the-floor beat.

VAN HALEN
OU812

1986
Van Halen issue *Live Without
a Net* concert video
November 24

1988
Van Halen's eighth album, *OU812*
May 20

1988
Van Halen headline
Monsters of Rock tour
May 27

1991
Eddie and Valerie welcome
Wolfgang
March 16

VAN HALEN BEST OF

VOLUME I

1995
Bad vibes for *Balance*,
Van Halen's tenth album
January 24

1996
Van Halen—with Dave—present
at MTV Video Music Awards
September 4

1996
The first compilation:
Best of Volume I
October 22

1998
Van Halen *III*, with Gary
Cherone as front man
March 17

2004
"Dimebag" Darrell buried with
one of Eddie's prized guitars
December 14

2006
Dave appears on bluegrass
Van Halen covers album
June 6

2007
Van Halen inducted into
Rock & Roll Hall of Fame
March 12

2007
Sammy sells majority of his
tequila business
May 7

1978
The band embarks on first tour
March 3

1978
Van Halen play Texxas Jam
July 1

1978
***Van Halen* certified platinum**
October 10

1979
Van Halen issue the rough 'n' tumble second album
March 23

1982
Eddie plays on Michael Jackson's *Thriller*
November 29

1983
The birth of 5150 Studios
January–December

1983
Van Halen headline the US Festival
May 29

1984
Van Halen score massive hit with *1984*
January 9

1985
Eddie inducted into Hollywood RockWalk
November 13

1986
Sammy replaces Dave for *5150*
March 24

1986
***5150* hits #1 on Billboard album charts**
April 25

1986
Dave issues *Eat 'Em and Smile*
July 7

1974
Van Halen is born
June

1976
Gene Simmons and Paul Stanley discover Van Halen
November 2

1977
Ted Templeman and Mo Ostin check out the band at the Starwood
February 2, 3

1978
Van Halen issue groundbreaking debut album
February 10

1980
Van Halen issue *Women and Children First*
March 26

1981
Eddie marries Valerie Bertinelli
April 11

1981
It's Eddie's album, *Fair Warning*
April 29

1982
The contentious fifth album, *Diver Down*
April 14

1984
The original Van Halen play their final show
September 2

1984
"Jump" wins Best Stage Performance at first MTV Video Music Awards
September 14

1985
Diamond Dave issues *Crazy from the Heat* . . . then quits Van Halen
January 28

1985
Eddie joins Sammy onstage at Farm Aid
September 22

1991
Putting in the work results in
For Unlawful Carnal Knowledge
June 17

1992
"Right Now" takes top prize at
MTV Video Music Awards
September 9

1993
The long-awaited first live album,
Live: Right Here, Right Now
February 23

1993
Longtime Van Halen manag
Ed Leffler dies
October 18

Fully six of the eleven songs proper are from *5150*, double-platinum by the time of the show and triple-platinum by the time the video came out on November 24, 1986. In (rearranged) order, interspersed with solo spots, we get "Summer Nights," "Get Up," ""5150,"" "Best of Both Worlds," "Love Walks In," and "Why Can't This Be Love," half of which were released as singles, with "Dreams" being the most surprising omission.

Visually, *Live without a Net* presents the band at their most cheery and primary-colored: Michael's wearing yellow, both Eddie and Sammy are in red parachute pants, with Eddie in a white tank top and Sammy going with various upper garb, including something akin to *Joseph and the Amazing Technicolor Dreamcoat*. His hair is long and bleached blond, and Michael is sporting a full beard. The performances are packed with energy, with Eddie, Alex, and Michael each taking an extended solo, with Michael playing his iconic Jack Daniels bass. Sammy's using a headset mic, so he's able to race around the large stage, with Eddie gamely keeping up, grinning, running on the spot, throwing out leg kicks, and regularly mugging with his new lead singer.

Live without a Net, initially issued as a VHS tape and LaserDisc, would sell double-platinum in the video category for sales of over two hundred thousand copies. In 2004, it saw re-release on DVD. Most saliently, it continues to live on YouTube, arguably a fashion disaster but also testimony to Van Halen very likely at their happiest.

Another shot from the New Haven show. The band included "I Can't Drive 55" in the set list.

26
MINE ALL MINE
VAN HALEN'S EIGHTH ALBUM, OU812

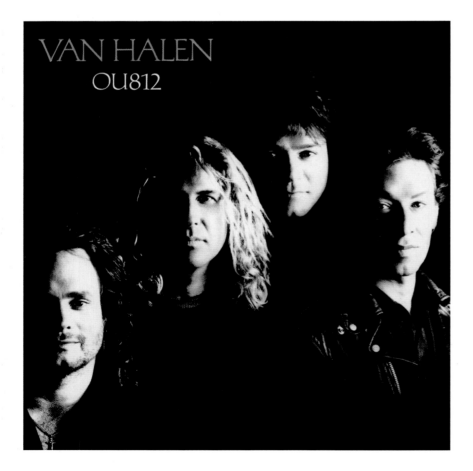

VAN HALEN
OU812

Demonstrating how Eddie and Sammy were still clicking, when it came time for Hagar to deliver a final contractually obligated studio album to Geffen, Eddie played bass and coproduced. *I Never Said Goodbye*, issued in 1987, went gold and gave Sammy a couple lasting solo songs in "Give to Live" and "Eagles Fly," the latter on which Eddie also plays guitar. Then it was time for a follow-up to 5150, the band working once again at Eddie's studio, no producer in sight, with Donn Landee getting a "Recorded by" credit.

Even with eight months at it, Sammy evidently didn't have much to say lyrically, and that's the first thing anybody complains about. Some also find the sound lacking in bottom end, but to my mind, that's because the first song, "Mine All Mine," specifically goes for that, and after that it's back to beefy enough.

Another change over 5150, the rockers on *OU812* (as in "Oh, you ate one, too") are more squarely rocking, with Eddie variably turning it up with respect to riffing, noodling, power chording, or otherwise placing guitar higher in the arrangement—I guess in other words, the parts are better. Most exemplifying this are "A.F.U. (Naturally Wired)," "Cabo Wabo," "Source of Infection," "Black and Blue," and "Sucker in a 3 Piece." Like last time—that is, no more and no less—there are two ballads of sorts, with "Feels So Good" and "When It's Love," both being appreciably up-tempo or at least driven by drums, again, just like last time.

This leaves three songs that are more or less outliers. "Finish What Ya Started," famously written by Sammy and Eddie on an impromptu jam at two in the morning, is a typical, twangy hair metal bluegrass lark, the type of which Van Halen invented across

a handful of comedy songs with Dave. "A Apolitical Blues" is a cover of an obscure Little Feat tune and does neither that fine band nor Van Halen justice, being a rote blues. It wasn't included on the vinyl (the record was appreciably quite long already, at forty-five minutes) but was included as a CD bonus track.

This leaves "Mine All Mine," inventive, exciting, and a song Sammy says he sweated blood over to get the lyrics, which are significantly serious and spiritual, especially against the hootin' and hollerin' and tossed-off sleaze of much of the rest. At the music end, Eddie and Alex collaborate on a sophisticated and buoyant rhythm, a mind meld of drums, guitars, and synths, while the solo section is possibly the greatest demonstration of the brothers being brotherly. The genius of this song is that it's written heavy metal and arranged pop.

OU812 zoomed up to triple-platinum within fourteen months of its May 20, 1988, release date and as of May 12, 2004, currently sits at four-times-platinum. Driving the happy numbers were the #5 placement of "When It's Love" and the #13 placement of "Finish What Ya Started," both of which also got bad fashion video treatment. Fan assessment of the album tends to be a bit negative, tainted by the fact that its two highest-value calling cards are a novelty song and a ballad with a despised and saccharine chorus. A revisit reveals piles and piles of action from Eddie, and like I say, "Mine All Mine" is a masterpiece.

Monsters of Rock, Giants Stadium. The bonus of hiring on Sammy was that he could support Eddie on guitar and generally fill in the sound.

EDDIE AND HIS KEYBOARDS

As discussed, Eddie and Alex got their grounding in music theory from piano, at the behest of their father, Jan Van Halen. It's an origin story to which many rock stars can relate. And like Eddie, many of those rock stars eventually followed a restless muse and explored keyboards as a way to expand the sound picture and palette of their records.

The Rolling Stones famously have lots of piano songs, although they never officially took on a keyboardist. John Paul Jones created many memorable keyboard parts for Led Zeppelin before passing the baton to Geddy Lee, who eventually took up keys as a big part of his job. Closer to home, Ronnie Montrose made synthesizers central to his post-Montrose band Gamma, most notably on the *3* album. ZZ Top watched *Eliminator* go diamond, in no small part due to the embrace of shiny new technologies. Freddie Mercury played the piano, and so did Steven Tyler.

And so did Eddie Van Halen. We've talked about how "And the Cradle Will Rock . . ." kicked off a relationship with the keys, although it would be a stretch to call this piano playing. As well, live onstage, Van Halen initially went the Led Zeppelin and Rush route and had the bass player deal with it for this initial curio, leaving Eddie to put bums in the seats doing what he did best. The next step was similarly novel and once more worlds away from Elton John or Billy Joel. The occasion is 1981's "One Foot Out the Door," where Eddie uses an Electro-Harmonix synthesizer to create the riff for what becomes a fast and pure heavy metal song, an oxymoron, given the circumstance. "Dancing in the Street" completes the trilogy of songs where Eddie smartly and yet reticently uses new technology to somewhat mimic what he might otherwise do on guitar.

The shocking change is "Jump," where Eddie now "plays" keyboards and, not only that, it sounds like keyboards. And it must be said that what is admirable, unlike the bands cited above, is the guitarist that is emerging as the band's keyboard player, a guitarist who happens to be the band's namesake as well as the world's most famed living practitioner of the instrument. On the same record, there's also opening instrumental "1984," which is a synthesizer showcase, and then "I'll Wait," which included multiple new tones over what we heard on side 1 as well as a synthesizer bass line.

Synthesized bass returns for "Why Can't This Be Love," with Eddie deftly integrating Oberheim OB-8 synth licks with guitar. The stakes are raised with "Love Walks In" and "Dreams," where you start to hear some actual percussive plinking piano—Eddie's using a MIDI-ed Steinway—although "Jump"-style synth notes dominate. There's a palpable sense of progress made, from the still crudely pastiched "Jump" through the more musical "I'll Wait" and into *5150*, where, as braying and '80s as it is, the new technology is blended with more sophistication, perhaps helped by the sympathetic electro-brightness applied to Alex's drums.

On *OU812*, "When It's Love" makes use of Oberheim, Yamaha, and Roland equipment plus the return of MIDI'ed grand piano in a re-creation of the *5150* sound, while "Feels So Good" feels good like "I'll Wait." Most intriguing is "Mine All Mine," where, as on "One Foot Out the Door," Eddie proposes a speedy hard rock proposition but challenging listeners to accept it with a synthesizer riff rather than guitar.

For Unlawful Carnal Knowledge is famously guitar-charged, but the album's linchpin song, "Right Now," features Eddie playing his purest and most purposeful piano yet, making it the focus of this highly promoted smash single just like he did with synthesizers on "Jump." This use of sincere, naked piano would continue with "Never Enough" from *Balance* and "Once" from *III*, with the culmination of Van Halen keyboard songs arriving up at the end of the *III* album. "How Many Say I" presents a vision of Eddie sitting at a piano like Freddie Mercury at the beginning of "Bohemian Rhapsody" and actually delivering a lead vocal—bravely but more than competently—across a contemplative and delicate song of essentially pure piano and nothing more.

Little did we know that this would also mark the end of Eddie playing keyboards. We'd get one more record from the band, *A Different Kind of Truth*, and of course the mandate there was to tear it up. "Tattoo" includes a synthesizer credit for Dave, but even that is incidental to the mayhem. Eddie would go out with all guns blazing, but also with his reputation bolstered due to the creative bravery it took to put aside his Frankenstrat and propose that keyboards might make his music more musical. It certainly paid off at the box office, with most of the songs discussed here becoming big hits, allowing the band to play for more and more fans at bigger and better shows, where, fortunately for us, there'd be more than enough howling guitar.

THE VAN HALEN ALBUM COVERS

I love reviewing album graphics, especially if I get to complain; and there's lots to complain about with this band, approximately on par with the likes of Foreigner, AC/DC, and Def Leppard. With that warning, here are the Van Halen wrappers ranked worst to first.

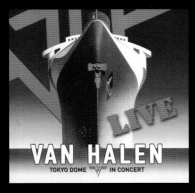

16. TOKYO DOME LIVE IN CONCERT

The assembly of the parts looks like a five-minute job by some kid with only a casual relationship with a PC's provided stock graphics program. And good luck giving the record a name, its title buried somewhere within the consecutive-reading, all-caps, and horrible-of-font VH LIVE VAN HALEN TOKYO DOME VH IN CONCERT.

15. BEST OF VOLUME I

Does Warner Bros. just hate us? Maybe that's it. Top row reads "VAN HALEN BEST OF" and bottom row reads—same dull font, smaller point size—"VOLUME I." There are two colors used, and there's a VH logo stuck in the middle in one of those colors, a cheap faux gold. That's a wrap.

14. FOR UNLAWFUL CARNAL KNOWLEDGE

Burgundy leather look, nice 3D rendering of the Van Halen "bracelet" logo, title in a classy font in gray. Not horrible, but also very little to it. More annoying in retrospect, given how much the *Best of Volume I* cover looks like a bootleg of this one. As Alex says, the guys wanted to keep it simple, just like the music.

13. II

The back and the inner sleeve are pretty cool, but the front is a bridge too far. I suppose with covers like this, you're supposed to focus on the music first and maybe burn a few brain cells on the logo, the brand. They're saying, "Our music is so good; let's have none of us waste time on pretty pictures." Back to the brand, *II* marks the birth of the pared-down, more utilitarian VH logo.

12. BALANCE

This is just creepy and dark, featuring anatomically unlikely, androgynous Siamese twin children on a seesaw, a ride that Siamese twins can't use. Alex has alluded to the cover representing the turmoil in the band at the time, along with the death of manager Ed Leffler.

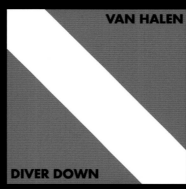

11. DIVER DOWN

Here we get a rendering of the caution flag used to indicate that there's a diver below the surface of the water. There's no logo, and the band name and album title are in the same dull-as-dishwater black all-caps font. The back cover is better, but it makes *Diver Down* look like a live album. We persist with the songs being listed in scrambled order.

10. THE BEST OF BOTH WORLDS

It had to get used eventually—namely, Eddie's iconic red, black, and white Frankenstrat design. Plus there's some effort put into the fonts, and the album title is unambiguous and even kinda decent for a compilation, especially given Van Halen's low bar for both titles and covers.

9. WOMEN AND CHILDREN FIRST

I dig the upscale forest-green and silver color palette, and the idea of using a small inset photo is quirky. But it's unforgivable that the Norman Seeff photo that was picked makes it look like Eddie has mutton chops like Tony McPhee from The Groundhogs. It's also kinda goofy, and the cover's got nothing to do with the title.

8. OU812

It's an homage to *Meet the Beatles*, but I prefer to think of it as a tribute to King Crimson's *Red*. I also appreciate the green, black, and white palette, recalling *Women and Children First*, and chuffed that the text on the original vinyl issue is embossed.

7. III

This is Frank "Cannonball" Richards doing his thing, with the implication being that one experiences Van Halen music in the gut. It's fitting with Alex's—should have mentioned this earlier, but album cover art was usually an Alex thing—sense of both humor and simplicity. As well, it perpetuates the band's regular use of black-and-white photography.

6. LIVE: RIGHT HERE, RIGHT NOW.

The house on the left was saved by Jesus, but no one can escape the hurricane of sound that is Van Halen live. I always thought the courier text at the top and the strange punctuation (and use of lowercase) made this look like a combination of bootleg and Sub Pop cover. Artsy stuff for a live album.

5. FAIR WARNING

Here we get a small detail from an intense psychological painting by Canadian prairies artist William Kurelek (1927–1972). The whole idea and outcome make for an enigmatic presentation at the level of Led Zeppelin. Four covers in, Van Halen are breaking rules; they have us thinking.

4. A DIFFERENT KIND OF TRUTH

The classy and muted color palette reminds me of *Women and Children First*. Sure, it's a stock photo, but the elements are arranged artfully, pleasing to the eye. Logo but no band name on the cover is interesting, as is that odd album title. Famously similar to the cover of the Commodores' *Movin' On* album from 1975.

3. 5150

Upscale, art-deco, luxurious . . . the Van Halen logo is resplendent in polished steel, wrapped around a shiny globe hoisted by Atlas, as depicted by Rick Valente from ESPN's *BodyShaping*. His bling tells us the album title. On the back, he's dropped the "egg" and out pops Van Halen 2.0.

2. VAN HALEN

Notwithstanding that Dave looks more like Jim Dandy than himself, here's a cover that captures the band not only in all their live performance glory but also oddly superstarry, given the upscale photography, red-hot blur lines and all. Also making us think Warner Bros. is serious about this band is the complicated logo, bolted down in the middle of the guys at work and at play.

1. 1984

The mischievous angel on the cover of *1984* was picked happenstance from the portfolio of Margo Nahas, who was asked to paint something else but was struggling with it. The fresh and memorable airbrushed shot—it's the child of one of Nahas's friends—will forever be compared with the cover of Black Sabbath's *Heaven and Hell*, which depicts three angels smoking.

27

RUNNIN' WITH THE DEVIL

VAN HALEN HEADLINE MONSTERS OF ROCK TOUR

Standing on top of the world, Van Halen quickly took it upon their shoulders that they tour as headliners on a festival bill called Monsters of Rock, named for the legendary one-off event in England but now Americanized and super-sized. Unfortunately, the trek turned out to be too big for the logistics to support it and it became a financial failure.

First off, reports estimated the stage at 350,000 pounds and seven stories tall, with a 50,000-pound, 850,000-watt lighting rig. And for sound? That's been pegged at 220,000 pounds and 250,000 watts, powered by two 40,000-pound generators and another 12,000-pound one for the trucks. There would have to be three revolving setups around the country to make everything happen on time, plus two roofing systems. Second, all of this would create a noisy long day out that would last nine hours, making it tough for kids to go to it on school days. Third, it would later be opined that the low ticket sales in some markets might be attributed to the fact that the new *OU812* record was just too new, having been issued a mere week before the first date.

The Monsters of Rock dance card kicked off with Lenny Wolf and his notorious Led Zeppelin—alikes Kingdom Come. Next came Metallica, odd band out with their uncompromising thrash sound after three albums, and actually the inspiration for much of the fan mayhem across the twenty-three-city, twenty-nine-date tour. Then came Dokken, established hair metal band with a guitarist and singer who despised each other, followed by Scorpions, who, as departing manager David Krebs warned the band at the time, was going look old and pasty by the end of their set in blinding sunlight. At least they were smart enough not to follow Metallica. That was left to Dokken, who suffered much abuse at the hands of the thrashing throngs.

Van Halen, of course, headlined, turning in a one-hundred-minute set each night (except for San Francisco's Candlestick Park, where there was a minor riot). But even they saw some bad luck, with Sammy falling off the stage at the very first gig, cracking his tailbone, and then losing his voice in Dallas. Multiple days saw food fights due to bad concessions, and a riot ensued in Miami after the show was stopped due to severe weather.

Typically, songs from the new album included "A.F.U. (Naturally Wired)," "Mine All Mine," "Cabo Wabo," "Finish What Ya Started," and "Black and Blue." From the old days, Sammy obliged with "Panama," "Runnin' with the Devil," "Ain't Talkin' 'bout Love," and Kinks cover "You Really Got Me." For a comedown, the band did a single ballad in "When It's Love," followed by the even quieter "Eagles Fly," featuring Sammy solo with an acoustic guitar.

Once the May, June, and July extravaganza ran its course, Van Halen did a more typical U.S. tour on their own, through October and November of that year. Into 1989, the band mounted a nine-date Tokyo campaign and then hit Hawaii on the way back, playing shows on February 4 and 5 in Honolulu. Europe would not get the tour, nor would Canada.

Sammy and Eddie jam on the closing night of Monsters of Rock.

28
LITTLE DREAMER
EDDIE AND VALERIE WELCOME WOLFGANG

Opposite: Eddie with Wolfgang tattoo, Los Angeles, 1995

The one and only child for both Eddie and Valerie Bertinelli, Wolfgang William Van Halen, was born on March 16, 1991, thereafter beginning life as a regular little California dude (if a privileged one) but quite soon growing into his own, rising to the reputation of both his first and last names. His birthday was subsequently celebrated for posterity by a cheery acoustic instrumental on *For Unlawful Carnal Knowledge* called "316," aptly placed between "Right Now" and "Top of the World," which is how Eddie obviously felt after the addition to the bloodline.

Wolfgang—or "Wolfie"—immediately bonded with dad over music, but it was Uncle Alex that first got him into the trade, teaching him a few things on the drums after watching him climb up and attempt to make some noise during band rehearsals. Wolfie took up the drums for real at the age of nine, with Dad getting him his first set the following year. He'd soon become proficient on guitar, bass, and keyboards, learning by ear just like Dad. Arguably and astoundingly, he'd be good enough to replace Michael Anthony in Van Halen by the age of sixteen, and not just barely. Far over on Dad's right, there'd be a third virtuoso with the Van Halen name in the band, one that must have had David Lee Roth wondering if he was back with his solo band listening to Billy Sheehan reimagine the bass.

In his new capacity, Wolfgang toured more than ably to the end, also appearing on *A Different Kind of Truth* and the *Tokyo Dome* live album, playing bass and performing backup vocals. In parallel he was making his own mark, first in Creed guitarist Mark Tremonti's band, Tremonti, joining as touring bassist, but then appearing on 2015's *Cauterize* and 2016's *Dust*. In 2021, Wolfie issued a seriously pure solo album under an adopted band name. *Mammoth WVH* would find Wolfgang playing all instruments and performing all vocals across a one-hour record of finely crafted heavy metal reflective of the creator's generation. The fourteen-track album would produce eight singles and rise to #12 on the Billboard charts, with Wolfgang putting together a band and touring the fine album, often in support of Guns N' Roses. The *II* record followed in August 2023, with Wolfgang now firmly ensconced as a significant part of the musical landscape, doing the most of any Van Halen alumni to carry on the brand.

But it hasn't been easy for Wolfgang. Although he's emerged from his father's shadow as a musical force and business and personality in his own right, he's long battled weight issues and just as publicly gotten into social media wars with haters and trolls, perhaps still hurting at dad's death, with a subtext being frustration at seeing the son flourish on his own and not continue with some imagined version of Van Halen, whether that be in a live forum or working with his Dad's vast archive of tapes. Critics should also never forget that Wolfgang had to watch, still as a child, the slow dissolution of his parents' marriage and then, at nineteen, the death of his mentor, hero, and father.

29
MAN ON A MISSION
PUTTING IN THE WORK RESULTS IN FOR UNLAWFUL CARNAL KNOWLEDGE

Sammy didn't "completely" get his way titling his third record with Van Halen (he was on his horse about censorship in rock and was brewin' for a fight), but he got his way with producers, bringing Ted Templeman back into the fold because he wasn't getting along with knobsman of choice Andy Johns of Led Zeppelin fame. So, it turns out both cats were involved, one essentially for vocals and the other to help Alex get a huge drum sound—he had asked Johns to dial in a snare sound similar to John Bonham's, but he also got shimmering, sizzling cymbals and a pounding bass drum attack to complete the circuit. As it would turn out, *F.U.C.K.* (as the album title is sometimes abbreviated) would represent the biggest, most panoramic Alex drum sound on record, although as a sacrifice, one that lacks in the various unique brown sound touchstones found elsewhere in the catalog.

Next, Eddie is playing his butt off, massaging in layer upon layer of sounds and sound effects, tunes, and tones (many of them astringent and Steve Howe–like, given a change in amplifiers) and putting aside keyboards, save for the iconic piano riff on "Right Now." The result is a record that is all about the brothers rocking out, with Sammy and Michael joining in and keeping up but, one imagines, slack-jawed at watching Eddie and Alex spin like two tops.

But out there in the world, the record was not universally viewed as a triumph. To be sure, it's heavy, long at fifty-two minutes, and lacking in extraneous pieces (save "316") or covers. But critics found Sammy's lyrics increasingly sophomoric and cocky, and they complained at the lack of particularly good songs and the diminished sense of technological experimentation that made *5150* and *OU812* quirky and fresh and even a little bit risky. Instead, what we got was dense and smothering, claustrophobic even.

The second of two nights at the Shoreline Amphitheatre, Mountain View, California, September 14, 1991. Supporting was Alice in Chains.

FOR UNLAWFUL CARNAL KNOWLEDGE
PHOTO/TV

KY102
KANSAS CITY'S HOME OF ROCK & ROLL
WELCOMES
VAN HALEN

SPECIAL GUEST: ALICE IN CHAINS
AUGUST 26, 1991
SANDSTONE AMPHITHEATER
KY102 COLLECTOR'S PATCH #8

That certainly describes opener "Poundcake," which begins with Eddie running an electric drill over his pickups. Once the band tumbles in, what we get is a thick wall of sound, one that essentially never lets up for the duration of the album to follow, save for "Right Now" and "316," delivered in succession near the end of what is a relentless and ear-fatiguing display of Van Halen on top.

In fact, the band was all too aware how on "Top of the World" they were. Sammy admits that it was hard to focus on work, with him and Eddie buying cars "every other day" and racing them up and down the highways of California. Despite the party atmosphere, the end result is indeed an album that sounds more deliberately crafted than the previous two and even *Balance*, with the critics going so far as to say it sounds labored or overworked. It definitely took a long time, with the band clocking in (sporadically) at 5150 from March 1990 through April 1991, with the album seeing issue on June 17 of that year.

But critics couldn't accuse the band of being poppy. If "Poundcake" wasn't the heaviest Van Hagar song to date, the next one, "Judgement Day," surely was, lethal of riff and beat black and blue by Alex. "Spanked" is slinky and lascivious but delivered with the same no-nonsense metal mix used across the album. "Runaround" goes a bit hair metal, but heavy hair metal, while "Pleasure Dome" is prog metal, with a spoken vocal and storyline very much like King Crimson's "Indiscipline" from *Discipline*. "In 'n' Out," "Man on a Mission," and "The Dream Is Over" continue the loud party until the cops come over and demand they play something nice, like "Right Now." After that we get "316," the minute-and-a-half acoustic guitar ode to Wolfgang, although this had been a preexisting piece of music that had even been played live. Last on offer is "Top of the World," framed upon a melodic and muted riff—barely a riff, more of a lick—that Eddie took out for a trial run as he was winding up the song "Jump" back on *1984*. Previous to that, live, you'd sometimes get it in "Dance the Night Away."

The sheer immensity of Van Halen at the turn of the decade, along with the success of the ponderous and philosophical "Right Now" as a beloved video, helped quickly push *For Unlawful Carnal Knowledge* to double-platinum status, with triple-platinum certification coming soon enough, in 1994. Getting "Poundcake" as an advance single might be credited with priming the pumps, with the effervescent delivery of the record on tour and the single release of "Top of the World" helping as well, just as the tour was getting underway. Most impressive was the fact that the album debuted at #1 on the Billboard 200 and stayed there for three weeks—and all of this with a crap album cover and no power ballads.

Eddie and Sam at the Orange County Speedway, Middletown, New York, July 6, 1993. Vince Neil supported across the United States in 1993.

30

THE DREAM IS OVER

"RIGHT NOW" TAKES TOP PRIZE AT MTV VIDEO MUSIC AWARDS

"Right Now" is a good song, both musically and lyrically, but not a great one. In fact, many Van Halen fans will have that debate with you about whether it's overrated. And the reason they can have that debate is because it's rated so highly, and that's because of the synergistic effect between what Sammy is saying in it and what director Mark Fenske says in it.

For his part, Sammy was proud of the lyrics, remarking that "I was tired of writing cheap sex songs," which, of course, ignores the fact that *For Unlawful Carnal Knowledge* had the usual dose of those. As for the music, that piano riff had been something Eddie had been working on all the way back to the *1984* album but could never get it sold to the rest of the guys (you can also hear the kernel of the idea in a piece of music Eddie made for a teen comedy called *The Wild Life*). As Sammy puts it, he was writing his carpe diem treatise, pondering the current state of the world as it were, while Eddie was retinkering the song in the other room. It then dawned on Sammy that they were writing the same song, and "Right Now" was born.

When it came time to do the video, Fenske had the idea to put in huge caps throughout the clip, more direct cultural and societal messages than what Sammy was saying, things like "Right now, blacks and whites don't eat together very much"; "Right now, the truth is being obscured"; "Right now, oil companies and old men are in control"; and "Right now, pigs are becoming lunch." Sammy thought the idea took away from his own meaning behind the song and, miffed, actually took off to South Carolina for a week and wouldn't answer phone calls.

It was only when Warner Bros. boss Mo Ostin rang him up and applied some pressure that he relented. But then Sammy had

Sammy admires one last trophy with the boys before he joins Cheap Trick.

to do the shoot with pneumonia and a sky-high fever, still angry but now also cranky from being sick. There's not a lot of band in the clip (which also irked Sammy), and at one point halfway through, Sammy is ostensibly supposed to be mouthing the words but just stands there impatient—which probably works even better, given the lofty artistic goals of the video. All the while Fenske, directing his first video, had to use family and crew members to get the shoot done on time and on budget.

At the 1992 MTV Video Music Awards, held in Los Angeles on September 9, 1992, "Right Now" went on to win for Best Direction in a Video, Best Editing in a Video, and also Video

of the Year, over Def Leppard, the Red Hot Chili Peppers, and Nirvana, the latter also having performed at the event. It was also nominated for Best Group Video, Best Metal/Hard Rock Video, and Breakthrough Video and was in the Viewer's Choice category.

Largely due to the heavy lifting of the video, "Right Now" has become the enduring song from the *For Unlawful Carnal Knowledge* album, regularly heard on classic rock radio, while "Poundcake" and "Top of the World" have faded. As for the video, despite Sammy's fit of pique at the time, he's gone on to soften about the experience, even reviving the concept for the title track from his 2008 solo album, *Cosmic Universal Fashion*.

31

ON FIRE

THE LONG-AWAITED FIRST LIVE ALBUM, LIVE: RIGHT HERE, RIGHT NOW.

Van Halen's first live album arose as somewhat of a necessity, a stickhandling of a sticky issue. Alex as a rule had always been against live albums, citing Led Zeppelin as the gold standard with respect to reticence (excepting *The Song Remains the Same* soundtrack album). But off to the side, David Lee Roth had been bugging Warner Bros. to put out a Van Halen hits package, even requesting that some of his solo songs be incorporated. Van Halen manager Ed Leffler managed to quell the idea by offering the label a live album, one that would include songs from the David Lee Roth era.

However, when *Live: Right Here, Right Now.* was issued as a double CD package on February 23, 1993, it was business as usual, with Van Hagar offering nothing more than "Ain't Talkin' 'bout Love," "Panama," "Jump," and the band's formative-years cover of "You Really Got Me" as bones thrown to Dave.

Also pretty standard were Sammy solo songs "One Way to Rock" and "Give to Live." The latter serves as Sammy's solo spot, so to speak, where he sings alone with acoustic guitar. Michael gets his own five-minute showcase, which includes Alex accompanying him on a bit of "Sunday Afternoon in the Park." The band launches into a brief instrumental version of "Pleasure Dome," after which Alex solos for a good nine minutes. "316" is the nominal title for Eddie's twelve-minute solo, where he chucks in bits of "Eruption," "Cathedral," and "Mean Street."

Elsewhere the biggest surprise is that there are only seven selections from *5150* and *OU812* combined, with fully eight *For Unlawful Carnal Knowledge* rockers getting beaten black and blue, huge drums captured by producer Andy Johns, with crowd noise relentless and loud like *Alive!* from Kiss back in 1975. The aforementioned nod at "Pleasure Dome" plus the inclusion of "The Dream Is Over" on the half-size video release of the album make it a running of the tables of sorts for the recent and surprisingly heavy album. Additional wrinkles come with a more electric version of "Finish What Ya Started" and a rousing rendition of The Who's "Won't Get Fooled Again," where Eddie plays Pete Townshend's iconic synthesizer part on guitar.

To construct the album, the band performed two dates deep into the epic F.U.C.K. tour—shows 100 and 101 of 109—at the Selland Arena in Fresno, California. But, as Sammy explains in his autobiography *Red*, the guys went crazy with the tapes, rerecording due to Eddie being out of tune and Alex varying with his tempos. All of a sudden Sammy's vocals are out of step, with Sammy divulging that he now found himself stuck in the vocal booth at 5150 with the video playing, having to resing the whole damn concert. Gamely taking care of it in one three-hour go, he was then periodically called back in to do further nitpicky fixes, further contributing to the fracture in band relations that would soon enough see him gone from the ranks.

Live: Right Here, Right Now. would quickly reach double-platinum certification in the United States, with the fourteen-track video version garnering a gold award for sales of more than fifty thousand copies. True to Alex's aversion for live albums, Van Halen wouldn't do another until *Tokyo Dome* way up into 2015. That makes for one double live album each from Sammy and Dave, with a notable void being anything from the classic Diamond Dave era circa 1978 to 1984.

32
WITHOUT YOU

LONGTIME VAN HALEN MANAGER ED LEFFLER DIES

Ed Leffler had been a mover and shaker in the entertainment business long before he started managing Sammy at the very beginning of his solo career, with Sammy taking him on in part because Leffler was California-based, representing a shift in the axis from his Montrose days and the passing of the torch from the East Coast style of management, which often came with ties to organized crime. In parallel, all through those years that Leffler had worked with Sammy, Noel Monk had been Van Halen's capable manager (Monk died in April 2022). When Sammy joined Van Halen, Leffler came with him, also capably managing the band and not in any way favoring Sammy, right up to his death on October 18, 1993, at the age of 57, due to throat and lung cancer, which had been diagnosed just two months prior.

His death shook Van Halen to the core. Leffler was a father figure to the guys, having worked with Petula Clark, The Carpenters, The Osmonds, Sweet, and Juice Newton. As Sammy Hagar band bassist Bill Church told me, on tour they'd run into the likes of Billy Martin and the governor of Hawaii, all of whom Leffler seemed to know on a first-name basis. Church also chuckled about a briefcase Leffler always had with him, stuffed with press clippings of his days with The Beatles. He remembers pranking Leffler by hiding his lighter, which was engraved with a personal message from John Lennon—Leffler, like Eddie Van Halen, was a chain smoker and was not against partaking in other things parties had to offer.

The loss of Leffler left a management void that, at first, resulted in chaos. Against Sammy's wishes, Alex tried to manage the band for a spell, with Eddie also getting involved. Once a search for proper representation took place, the band settled on Ray Danniels and his SRO Management company out of Toronto, known for managing Rush since the beginning. Danniels was married to Alex's wife's sister, making him a brother-in-law. Immediately a rift formed, with Alex and Eddie siding with Danniels and Sammy never to be satisfied with the new arrangement.

The *Balance* album of 1995 would bear a dedication to Leffler that reads, "Ed Leffler—There wasn't much he missed in life." Alex's shocking choice of cover art, featuring a Siamese twins image of sorts representing the good and bad of life and a yearning for harmony, was also in part inspired by Leffler's passing. In further tribute to their manager, Eddie had taken an old song he had written about a friend's suicide and repurposed it for Leffler as "Crossing Over," used as a bonus track for the Japanese issue of *Balance*—Eddie's original guide vocal can still be heard behind Sammy's contribution. As Church relates, Sammy, who has an interest in UFOs and the paranormal, has told him that even though Leffler had crossed over, he and Leffler still communicate regularly.

33

SOURCE OF INFECTION

BAD VIBES FOR *BALANCE*, VAN HALEN'S TENTH ALBUM

Le Zenith, Paris, May 24, 1995

Amid battles over management following Ed Leffler's death, Eddie cutting his hair and quitting drinking, and Sammy's divorce from Betsy, Van Halen found themselves grinding it out for three months of eight-hour days, trying to get a full record of material together at the nicotine-stained insane asylum called 5150. Indicative of the growing divide, most of Sammy's vocals would have to be recorded at Little Mountain in Vancouver, domain of the producer on the album, Bruce Fairbairn.

Balance would be issued January 24, 1995, and the response would be underwhelming. Gone were the action-packed songs and the swagger and heft of *For Unlawful Carnal Knowledge*. Instead, what we got was a somewhat limp salad bar of sounds that would come off as half *OU812* and half *Diver Down*. The *Diver Down* comparison comes from the inclusion of three instrumental pieces. "Strung Out" and "Doin' Time" were brief and innocuous enough, but "Baluchitherium," at four minutes, came off as a bad song without lyrics, a symptom of trouble. In fact, Sammy's inability to come up with lyrics for the track was just another log on the fire toward his firing. It would be left off the vinyl issue of the album, due to time constraints.

Elsewhere, Eddie was annoyed that for "Amsterdam," an acceptable crunchy rocker dedicated to the birthplace of the brothers, Sammy decided to riff about pot being legal there. "Big Fat Money," a sort of "Teenage Nervous Breakdown" redux—in other words, a fast boogie jam—sported even worse words. Taking up prime real estate as the second song on the album, primary single "Can't Stop Lovin' You" was a maudlin composite of every time previous the band wrote an up-tempo pop ballad. Poppier yet and equally inconsequential was "Not Enough," a true (and rote) power ballad, distinguished by Eddie going back to the piano. Also quiet, "Take Me Back (Deja Vu)" nonetheless finds the band in fresh acoustic guitar mode, kind of casual and Zeppelin-esque, proving that they could rise above and exude chemistry even on a light song, in this case a "campfire"-type thing.

Still, despite cruising at a multitude of altitudes, "The Seventh Seal," "Don't Tell Me (What Love Can Do)," and "Feelin'" all succeeded at dark introspection, with Van Halen, through an analysis of their own problems, unwittingly coming off as relevant in the grunge era, even if the Seattle scene was already on the wane at this juncture. Which brings up a point: The deliverance of

a Van Halen album in 1995 came off as untethered from reality or usefulness. This wasn't the age of the guitar hero, or of lyrics like "Amsterdam" or "Big Fat Money," or of Fairbairn productions and power ballads like "Can't Stop Lovin' You." In effect, it just seemed like a weird time to get a Van Halen record, or an AC/DC record for that matter, with *Ballbreaker* arriving later that year, also mixed by Mike Fraser for a further connection to Vancouver.

But if you were inclined to accept the premise, you were confronted with convincingly aggressive and pretty much universally lauded songs like "Don't Tell Me (What Love Can Do)" and "Aftershock," both indicative, again, of the brown sound chemistry that occurs when these four guys get together. Add in the adjacent "Humans Being" and "Crossing Over" and there's an argument to be made that we were just a few shuffled cards away from *Balance* becoming noble.

As we'd find out, the record deserved comparisons to *A Different Kind of Truth* as well, with the intro to "Take Me Back (Deja Vu)" drawing from that of a predebut song called "No More Waiting," and with the "Amsterdam" riff being heard as far back

as 1985. There's also Eddie remarking, somewhat bafflingly, that "The Seventh Seal" was written before Van Halen was even a band. And even if the track earned the guys a (random) Grammy nomination in the Best Hard Rock Performance category, it's one that divides the fans. A wall of sound is created, to be sure, but the sort of stated combined narrative of Eddie being philosophical about his struggle for sobriety, and Sammy playing the religious mystic . . . we really don't think about either of these guys this way.

Still, Van Halen could not be denied, with the album almost immediately going double-platinum, en route to a triple-platinum designation in 2004. It was also the band's fourth album in a row to hit #1 on the Billboard 200, driven by two successful early singles: first, "Don't Tell Me (What Love Can Do)," and in March of '95, "Can't Stop Lovin' You." In fact, first-week sales were even more robust that those of *For Unlawful Carnal Knowledge*. The live campaign also helped the band move units, with the guys jokingly rechristening it the Ambulance tour, due to Eddie's hip issues (resulting in hip replacement surgery) and Alex having to play drums in a neck brace.

Munich, Germany,
June 3, 1995

National Stadium,
Arms Park, Cardiff, Wales,
June 21, 1995

MEET & GREET

VAN HALEN
BALANCE
NORTH AMERICA
ARENA TOUR 1995

VAN HALEN
BALANCE
NORTH AMERICA
AMPHITHEATRE TOUR 1995

WORKING
PERSONNEL

Act Three
TROUBLE

First show of the reunion
tour with Dave, Bobcats
Arena, Charlotte, North
Carolina, September
27, 2007

34
BALLOT OR THE BULLET

VAN HALEN—WITH DAVE—PRESENT AT MTV VIDEO MUSIC AWARDS

It was a debacle reminiscent of Kiss on *Tomorrow with Tom Snyder*, where Gene Simmons and Paul Stanley stared daggers into a slightly tipsy Ace Frehley, who proceeded to yuk it up and steal the spotlight from the supposed stars of the show. The occasion was the MTV Video Music Awards on September 4, 1996, at the Radio City Music Hall in New York City, and the original lineup of Van Halen was asked to show up together to announce the winner in the Best Male Video category, with Beck being the winner.

Or Van Halen being the loser, depending on how you want to look at it, and even Beck losing out, given how his achievement had been overshadowed by the publicity stunt. And, boy, does Diamond Dave love a publicity stunt. The real reason for them being there was to announce a reunion of the classic lineup, materially demonstrated by the following month's release of *Best of Volume I*, which would include two new songs with Dave singing.

Things were imbalanced (vis-à-vis Beck) right from the start, with the band introduced in typical elliptical style by Dennis Miller, after which the guys saunter onstage to "Runnin' with the Devil" over the PA accompanied by a prolonged bout of applause. Dave wanders around the stage soaking in the adulation, evidently really pleased with being him, as the rest of the guys dutifully line up at the podium. Eddie starts to do the job at hand, and Dave interrupts him, making the announcement that this was the first time the band had stood onstage together for over a decade, which is not that announcement-worthy, less so given the circumstance. Eddie begins again and turns the next line over to Michael, but Dave interrupts again and rambles about how things are so different since the good ol' "I want my MTV" days, dropping an F-bomb in the telling.

Eddie grabs Dave's shoulders and proceeds to crowd him out as they watch the clips of the nominees—namely, Bryan Adams, Seal, and Beck, with R. Kelly perhaps representing a bad omen, and Coolio, too, dead in 2022 at the age of 59. They get through that okay, and then Dave announces the winner, a little over the top but he means well. Beck comes up and plays it completely straight, delivering the polar opposite of a Dave spiel. The contrast is indeed palpable, with Beck closing off with "I don't know what to say. I never won one of these before." And where is Dave? He's behind Beck doing a shimmy and shake and basically not paying attention.

Afterward backstage, Eddie and Dave nearly come to blows, although they manage to hold it together for at least one breezy enough interview. Actually, the most dramatic moment is when Eddie flashes his brother a mean look, when Alex lets slip that the interviewer's use of the word "happy" (concerning the situation in Van Halen) might be going a bit far. All told, the unfortunate appearance reversed the jets on what was supposed to be a full-on reunion, again, kicked off by the two new compilation tracks. Instead, eleven years would pass before the guys would patch things up, and they'd even get a record out. But yeah, a decade of what could have been was lost in less than five minutes of Dave being a goofball and hogging the limelight.

"Believe me, we're as surprised as you are."

35

BIG FAT MONEY

THE FIRST COMPILATION: BEST OF VOLUME I

Warner Bros. had been itching to do a Van Halen greatest hits album for a while. Now with Sammy having left the band, it seemed like as good a time as any to sum up the state of affairs thus far. After David Lee Roth had called him up and asked about the forthcoming compilation, Eddie came up with the idea of the guys working together again. Eddie had made solid tentative steps on his sobriety, working with a therapist who had gotten him into yoga and some visualizing exercises, the result being that he had written three songs in an hour, or five songs in a day, depending on the telling. One of those, he says, was "Me Wise Magic." After he'd thought about the situation and discussed it with Alex and Michael, he came up with a plan to do five songs together and pick the best two to go on the compilation as bonus tracks.

Best of Volume I would emerge on October 22, 1996, and feature eight old chestnuts with Dave, six catalog tracks from the Sammy years, plus "Humans Being," also a Sammy song, from the *Twister* soundtrack. Then there was "Me Wise Magic" and "Can't Get This Stuff No More" to get everybody talking. Trouble is, once Eddie had narrowed it down to the two new songs, he realized that he wasn't particularly enamored with Dave's lyrics. Eddie then tried to get Dave to sing some words brought in by producer Glenn Ballard, who literally brought him to the studio song doctor Desmond Child. Having that crash in flames, Dave then performed a hasty rewrite, with the track ultimately credited to the classic Van Halen lineup. As for "Can't Get That Stuff No More," as Sammy tells the story, that was a rewrite of a *Balance* reject called "Back Door Shuffle," which resulted in Sammy getting overnighted a check for $35,000 from manager Ray Danniels in order to let it happen.

"Me Wise Magic" turned out to be a rhythmic and exciting enough Van Halen rocker with an ebullient wall-of-sound chorus, but "Can't Get This Stuff No More" is pretty much an amplified version of "Secrets" from *Diver Down*, a shuffle like the original title would suggest, with Dave taking the opportunity to vamp like he's on a stripper pole. "Humans Being" was a dark and pounding rocker somewhat akin to "Don't Tell Me (What Love Can Do)." It's the last song Sammy ever worked on with Van Halen, and the guys predictably butted heads over the lyrics. What's cool about this version is that it's 5:14 long, whereas the *Twister* release was a 3:28 single edit. The production credit goes to Bruce Fairbairn, with Ballard getting the credit on the two new Roth songs. Engineering on both is Dutch musician Erwin Musper, famed for his work with Def Leppard, Scorpions, and Bon Jovi.

Warner capitalized on latent demand for a Van Halen greatest hits album, with *Best of Volume I* certifying at triple-platinum as of the big-basket accounting that management did with the Recording Industry Association of America on May 12, 2004, while easily picking up another million in sales from the major markets around the world. Quite surprisingly, none of the three extant tracks did much at radio, fading quickly and not enduring in later live sets.

Eddie at the Jason Becker
Benefit at Chicago's Riviera
Theatre, November 17, 1996

36
NOT ENOUGH
VAN HALEN III, WITH GARY CHERONE AS FRONT MAN

One supposes that Van Halen's eleventh album, issued March 17, 1998, was doomed from the start—or at least predisposed and primed for doom—given the bad blood building between band and fan over the debacles with both lead singers previous. It wasn't out of the question, though, that Eddie could triumph. To be sure, Gary Cherone was a hire of convenience, given that Extreme had been under the SRO Management banner. As well, he's coming in just as hot as Sammy did, with lots of goodwill as a smart guy, powerful voice, and successful recording artist in his own right, given Extreme's notching of a double-platinum album and another one at gold for good measure.

The trouble is that Eddie's music had to be unassailable, and it wasn't. Dealing with his newfound sobriety and feeling philosophical and reflective—he'd even been reading up on Buddhism—Eddie was digging down deep and resurfacing with music that was, at times, atmospheric and ambient and, when rocking, sort of jammy with obscure purpose, willfully ragged, as if he were asking us not to think about songs but to focus on the guitar and the wiry, briny pickle sounds that it can make.

Fleet Center, Boston, May 21, 1998. Supporting on the night was Kenny Wayne Shepherd.

At the outset he was pumped. Gary would come ready with things to say, whereas in the past, Eddie'd usually have some music ready and be begging Dave or Sammy to write something, preferably something smart. So, he had this inspired relationship going with Gary, although not with Michael (who plays on only three tracks on the album) nor particularly with Alex, it seems, or with a strong producing voice, going with a buddy in Mike Post and essentially coproducing the album with him. Eddie even sings a song, "How Many Say I," which unfairly attracted barbs—the sentiments are noble, and Eddie's vocals are really good, almost as if this guy missed his calling! I'm kidding, of course (he obviously found and embraced his calling), but yes, he can sing. The problem is that this was one of four lengthy soft rock songs on the album, with a couple more being poppy (and casual), leaving essentially three to be heavy (and casual). In fact, all told, at 65 minutes, III is the band's longest album and yet even its shortest songs seem gratuitous, and that's before we even get to two pointless instrumentals in "Neworld" and Primary."

At the rocking end, "Ballot or the Bullet" is commendable all 'round, featuring lots of guitar, Alex's best drumming, and then meaningful lyrics from the Bostonian. Lead single "Without You" is adequate but, again, kind of a shambles, with simple parts that seem stuck together with duct tape. Adding to the perceived failure of the album, the video for it, shot in both Los Angeles and at the Icehotel in Sweden, cost over $1 million, and, although it made #1 on the Billboard sub-chart Mainstream Rock, it also faded into obscurity fast. "Fire in the Hole" is typical "Van Hagar" music to welcome, while "From Afar" manages an interesting alloy of both electric and atmospheric. Michael's not on "Ballot or the Bullet," but he's on these latter three, remarking after the fact that not only did it feel like a solo album from Eddie but that the boss was dictating to him what to play on the bass.

As metaphor for the idea that unwise artistic decisions were being made at every turn, a song called "That's Why I Love You" was left off the project, with many fans now calling it the best thing this lineup did together. But even that's a pop rocker, with chord changes and reliance on rhythm guitar more than any structure that might come from a riff.

The III album, purely by virtue of the change in singers being big news, got to #4 on the Billboard 200 but never got past a gold certification in the United States. Plans for a follow-up, with Danny Kortchmar producing, were suspended after the bad reviews and a lackluster response to the band on tour, with Gary shortly thereafter excused from his duties, almost with apologies. For his part, Gary rues the fact that the band didn't mount a tour playing all the old classics before they embarked on making the record. He figures this would have gotten people used to his presence. After all, he had rather thespian stage moves, was notably lacking in long blond hair, and wasn't even from California but, rather, Boston, about as far from a Diamond Dave state of mind as possible while still being part of the lower forty-eight.

But like I say, it wasn't that he wasn't a respected figure in hard rock, and as a bonus, his voice bore a resemblance to Sammy's. To be sure, that might have helped, but like I say, Eddie just didn't come with strong songs and nor did Alex come with a particularly strong album cover, notwithstanding how ill-matched it was to the confusing title. In other words, all the ducks had to be in a row for Van Halen to pull off yet another change of front man, and other than a pretty good pick in Gary Cherone for the lightning rod role, there were no ducks.

This page and opposite: More scenes from the venerable Pine Knob, northwest of Detroit, September 3, 1998

37

TOP OF THE WORLD

VAN HALEN AND 1984 CERTIFIED DIAMOND

The Recording Industry Association of America's gold certification award goes back to 1958, essentially the birth of rock 'n' roll. But the platinum level was invented only in 1976, with multiplatinum to follow in 1984. On March 16, 1999, a swanky party was held at the Roseland Ballroom in Midtown Manhattan, New York City, to announce a new level of distinction—namely, the diamond certification, celebrating sales in excess of ten million copies of an album. On hand for the event were Elton John, Kenny Rogers, Kenny G., Billy Joel, and MC Hammer, along with members of AC/DC, Boston, Guns N' Roses, Metallica, Def Leppard, Journey, Boyz II Men, Led Zeppelin, and ZZ Top.

Unsurprisingly, Eddie and Alex weren't part of the festivities— Dave sure would have had some fun—but they were emphatically part of the counting and accounting. Of the forty-six artists feted at the event, only The Beatles, Garth Brooks, Mariah Carey, The Eagles, Whitney Houston, Elton John, Pink Floyd, Bruce Springsteen, somebody called Various Artists, and the heroes of our story, Van Halen, had more than one reason to be there. On August 7, 1996, the band's self-titled debut had surpassed the ten million mark, and much more recently, on February 8, 1999, *1984* had joined *Van Halen* at this esteemed level of success, not yet formalized until five weeks later at the Roseland.

Rifle through the alphabet, from AC/DC through to ZZ Top, and you'll find that this achievement has eluded all but a few artists, even if *Back in Black* has shifted more units than Van Halen's two diamond records combined. It's testimony to the magic of the original lineup, and it's also testimony to the fact that fiery, heavy metal rock 'n' roll can transcend its perceived limitations and permeate to the core of pop culture, so long as the artistic intentions behind the caterwauling din are pure and powerful.

Although *Van Halen* and *1984* have not been recertified past ten-times-platinum status—and indeed have not been reexamined since the March 1999 diamond certification party—a handful of Van Halen awards were refreshed in 2004 (and no further). These include *5150*, *OU812*, *Balance*, and the band's two compilations. Curiously, only Van Halen *II* from the David Lee Roth era was included in the May 12, 2004, cull, recertifying at an impressive five-times-platinum despite the absence of a career-defining runaway hit single.

The brothers at the height of Van Halen mania, 1984

38

RIGHT NOW

EDDIE ANNOUNCES HE IS FIGHTING CANCER

On top of the hip replacement surgery Eddie had done in 1999, due to his rambunctious stage performances, and the pain he'd been experiencing since 1995 due to chronic avascular necrosis (death of bone tissue; one of the causes is alcoholism), it turns out that Eddie had been dealing with tongue cancer since 2000.

On April 19, 2001, David Lee Roth posted a statement on his website intimating that a reunion with the band was all systems go. This was followed by a statement on April 26 from Eddie on the official Van Halen site that read, "I'm sorry for having waited so long to address this issue personally. But cancer can be a very unique and private matter to deal with. So, I think it's about time to tell you where I'm at. I was examined by three oncologists and three head-and-neck surgeons at Cedars Sinai just before spring break and I was told that I'm healthier than ever and beating cancer. Although it's hard to say when, there's a good chance I will be cancer-free in the near future. I just want to thank all of you for your concern and support. Love, Eddie."

Dave responded the next day with, "I was stunned this morning to learn Eddie Van Halen has cancer. My condolences. You can whip this, champ. See ya down the road, D."

Meanwhile, in a grim turn of events, three weeks after the 2001 statement, on May 18, Eddie and Wolfgang were at an LAPD charity golf tournament and Eddie was, by all accounts, pretty boozed up and chain-smoking the whole time. In other words, his demons continued to plague him, and perhaps there was a tinge of fatalism involved as well. In any event, it reminds one of Valerie's complaints that, cancer or not, Eddie was not taking care of himself.

For his part, Eddie opined in 2015 that he might have gotten cancer from holding his picks in his mouth—picks that were made from brass and copper—due to the exact location of the cancer. He qualified that it was just a theory of his but that his doctors (he had been getting treatment at the University of Texas M.D. Anderson Cancer Center in Houston, as well as Cedars Sinai in Los Angeles) deemed it not out of the question. He also reflected on the fact that he basically lives in a recording studio "filled with electromagnetic energy" and that he was "smoking and doing a lot of drugs and a lot of everything."

The diagnosis resulted in Eddie having a third of his tongue removed. He was subsequently declared cancer-free, issuing a statement in May 2002 that read, "I wanted to let you all know that I've just gotten a 100 percent clean bill of health—from head to toe. I wanted to share the good news with you immediately. And of course, I thank you all for all your good wishes and prayers along the way. Now it's time to really get back to the music and fun . . . so party on and you'll be hearing from us very soon."

39
HOUSE OF PAIN

DAVID AND SAMMY'S SOLO BANDS MOUNT A TOUR

It was about as improbable as a reality TV show about Ozzy Osbourne and his family, or more conceptually adjacent, Paul Rodgers fronting Queen. What we're talking about is a weirdly named tour called Song for Song, The Heavyweight Champions of Rock and Roll, commencing May 29, 2002, featuring Dave and his solo band co-headlining a tour with Sammy and his solo band, flipping slots night to night until the whole thing became too much. As Sammy put it in his autobiography *Red*, he and über-manager Irving Azoff came up with the idea "just to piss off Van Halen and get the fans worked up."

Right from the outset, the passive-aggressive insults were chucked like darts to the heart of the matter, beginning with Diamond Dave on the Howard Stern show with Sammy phoning in, the idea being that they would do a coin toss to sort out who would headline the first show in Cuyahoga Falls near Cleveland. Along with rapid-fire and witty barbs directed at each other, both front men unloaded on the Van Halen brothers for their inactivity at the time.

Once the show—colloquially referred to as Sam and Dave, or more amusingly, Sans Halen—got on the road, there were two different philosophies at work. As Sammy would remind any classic rock jock that would listen, he had a well-defined solo career, and this was sort of an extension of that. Ergo, he was out with the Waboritas doing his Jimmy Buffet thing. A typical Sammy set would include "Shaka Doobie (The Limit)," "Runaround," "Three Lock Box," "There's Only One Way to Rock," "Top of the World," "Right Now," "Best of Both Worlds," "Why Can't This Be Love," "Finish What Ya Started," "Eagles Fly," "I Can't Drive 55," "Heavy Metal," "Mas Tequila," "When It's Love," and "Dreams." In other words, he loaded in a little more Van Hagar, but he wanted the crowd to know that he was his own man, too.

On the other hand, Dave didn't have much going on at the time, so his presentation was a little more custom-built. For a band, he repeated the formula used for *Eat 'Em and Smile*, *Skyscraper*, *A Little Ain't Enough*, and *DLR Band*—namely, the assembly of a baby robot lord version of Van Halen. Only this time it would be pointedly purpose-built: A typical Dave set list would include "Hot for Teacher," "Panama," "And the Cradle Will Rock . . . ," "Mean Street," "Dance the Night Away," "Runnin' with the Devil," "I'm the One," "You Really Got Me," "Beautiful Girls," "So This is Love?," "Atomic Punk," "Little Dreamer," "(Oh) Pretty Woman," "D.O.A.," "Yankee Rose," "Ice Cream Man," "Everybody Wants Some!!," "Ain't Talkin' 'bout Love," and "Jump." In other words, even though Sammy proclaimed that he was out to put Dave in his place every night, it was Dave who stacked the deck toward that goal, filling his action-packed slot with crowd-pleasers.

Michael Anthony would be Sammy's guest from time to time, with Gary Cherone jumping onstage when the tour swung through the Extreme legend's hometown of Boston. Additionally, Sammy had floated the idea of Dave and himself singing a few songs together, but that was rejected by Dave, with Sammy reading the tea leaves and realizing that for Dave, this was a flat-out competition. In Detroit, Kid Rock seemed to have brokered a deal, but then Dave backed out, claiming a sore throat, which didn't fly as an excuse on all the ensuing occasions Sammy pounded on his door and tormented Dave to keep his promise.

One would have to say that, in the end, Sammy prevailed, despite less impressive songs. The goodwill built up by The Wabos and the good vibes emanating from Sammy made for more of a fun night out against the cult of Dave and a bunch of fast guns nobody knew, although, of course, guitarist Brian Young, bassist James LoMenzo, and drummer Ray Luzier are no slouches.

The tour was an American campaign exclusively, with the guys jousting their way through all of June and August, along with three dates in July. By the end of it, Dave and his entourage of bodyguards had built a bad-will wall around their fearless leader to the point where all niceties between the costars and between their crews and security had gone out the tour bus window. In fact, a couple of dates at the end had to be canceled, attributed to Sammy falling ill.

"It could have been a great thing," Sammy told me. "And maybe it could have led to the Sam and Dave show with Van Halen, and that would've been the ultimate for the Van Halen fans and ultimate for everybody. You want to talk about the biggest tour in the world, there you go. But Dave blew it, and so that will never happen and I'll never work with the guy again, and that's just the way it goes (laughs). So, in hindsight, I wouldn't have done it; it was a waste of time."

Promoting the tour at the Sky Bar in Los Angeles

40

TAKE ME BACK (DEJA VU)

FIVE-MONTH TOUR FINDS THE BAND REUNITED WITH SAMMY

It had been six years since Van Halen had played live, and Eddie had not taken it well. There was his new battle with cancer but also at the same time his ongoing battle with drugs, alcohol, and nicotine. Oblivious to this, Sammy first contacted Alex on a whim, in an attempt to bury the hatchet. Next came a visit to 5150 where Sammy first got a glimpse at just how rough Eddie was. Nonetheless, a plot was hatched between the guys and Irving Azoff to put the band back on the road.

The first hurdle was what to do with Michael. The brothers had been resentful of Michael staying friends with Sammy during the rift of the late '90s and initially didn't want him in the band. With Sammy insisting on his presence, Michael was forced to accept a drastic pay cut as a musician for hire, along with forgoing his rights to the Van Halen name along with other concessions. He reluctantly took the deal because he thought it would be the last time the band would play together. The second hurdle came with Sammy's intentions to promote his Cabo Wabo tequila brand on the tour, against the wishes of the brothers. Michael divulged that Sammy had independently made deals with venues to sell the brand, which had irked Eddie and Alex. In defiance, Sammy got a Cabo Wabo tattoo and wore short sleeves.

But all of this might have been overcome if Eddie had been looking after his health. As Sammy frames it, Eddie was hunched over, alarmingly skinny and bedraggled, missing part of his tongue due to cancer but also missing teeth.

"Some of the shows were some of the greatest shows we ever did," Sammy told me of the ill-fated tour kicked off on June 11, 2004, in Greensboro, South Carolina. "Some of them weren't so hot. Believe me, there were nights where I just wanted to walk off the stage and say, 'I'm sorry' (laughs). But it was the in-between activities, the traveling together, the trying to get in the same room and work out what we were going to do, and if there was going to be a future, and what my ideas were for the future of Van Halen,

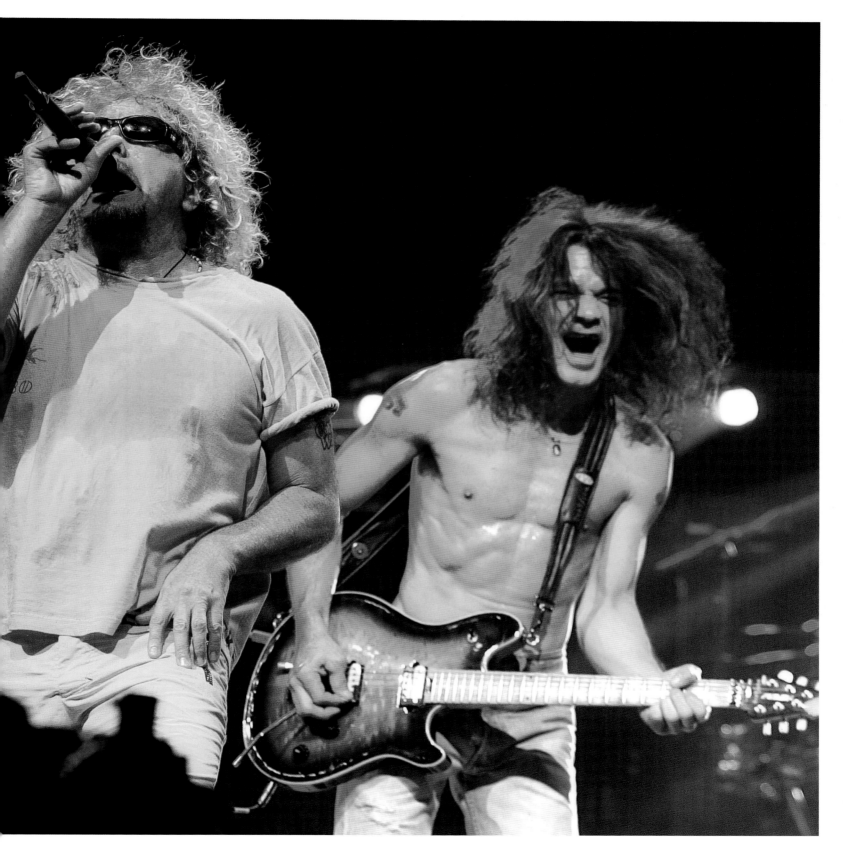

and what Eddie's ideas were for the future of Van Halen . . . there were a lot of problems there, let me tell you. It was just impossible (laughs). So, it really made the whole thing strenuous. It ended up, I had my own airplane and Eddie had his own airplane. I mean, it was that stupid. Because we would fight. They would have to drag us off each other. And, you know, I'm the most fun-loving, good-time guy on the planet, man. I'm all about, hey, how much fun can we have here? And he's like, well, how miserable can we make everyone? I just couldn't sit back and let that happen. I was always the guy who would step in and everyone else just kind of said, 'Back off,' and I'm just not that kind of person."

"He seemed to like being on the road," asserts Sammy, "but he would destroy his hotel room and he would try to bust the window out of a plane at forty thousand feet with a wine bottle and stuff. It wasn't about being on the road. It was about what Eddie was doing with his own personal life. He was on a very self-destructive trip and trying to take everyone around him down with it. It just wasn't user-friendly. His brother, who is a wonderful human being, you know, fought with the guy daily. I mean, he wouldn't play the songs right. Some nights you couldn't even recognize the song, wrong key, and he just wasn't being much of a professional out there. He was in pretty bad shape."

Still, as I told Sammy, I saw the show in Toronto on July 3, and it was smokin'. In fact, on many nights, Eddie could rally and turn in a transcendent performance, although lots of video is on record showing Eddie screwing up, most notably during his long solo spotlights. And yet the guys managed to hold it together for fully five months and do eighty-three shows, selling more than a million tickets and grossing $54.3 million, making it the sixth biggest tour of the year. But, as Sammy says, it was grueling, plagued with a definite split between Michael and him on one side and the brothers on the other, with, as he explains in his book, "different jets, different hotels, different limos and different security details."

As for the set list, there were many interesting wrinkles, including early classics like "Somebody Get Me a Doctor" and (occasionally) "Runnin' with the Devil," along with the new songs off the current *The Best of Both Worlds* compilation—namely, "Up for Breakfast," "It's About Time," and "Learning to See." Most obscure was "Deeper Kind of Love" from Sammy's 2000 solo album, *Ten 13*.

During the second of two performances in Tucson, Arizona, November 19, 2004, at the end of a grueling night, a shirtless Eddie proceeded to smash his guitar and hurl it dangerously skyward, not in an expression of energy or joy but in anguish and frustration. Sammy calls Tucson "the worst show we've ever done in our lives." Fans call it Black Friday. Neither Sammy nor Michael would ever play with the band again.

More shots from the two-night homestand in LA. Support on the night was Shinedown, who had been with the band since July 19 in Chicago.

DAVE VS. SAMMY: THE SOLO CAREERS

One thing that is crazy from the heat about what Dave managed to do outside of Van Halen versus what Sammy has accomplished is that both these guys had about the same amount of significant success. Everything else is wildly divergent.

Looking at Sammy first, to be chronological, he went solo after two albums with Montrose, the first of which long after went platinum. Through fully five albums on Capitol, Sammy didn't sell much but was in the game, supporting on large tours, being the sandwich band on three-band bills and headlining in his hot markets, like St. Louis. A jump to Geffen in 1982 sent *Standing Hampton* platinum, *Three Lock Box* gold, and *VOA* platinum up into 1984. As for his sound, it was a sort of Midwest, heartland hard rock, a bit of experimentation to the left and some heavy metal to the right. Picture John Mellencamp or Bryan Adams with more riffs, and then at the end, with *VOA*, we're in a sort of radio-friendly hair metal zone, an update on Loverboy and Night Ranger.

Next comes the Hagar Schon Aaronson Shrieve supergroup album and, while inside of Van Halen, in 1987, *I Never Said Goodbye*, which goes gold. Once freed from the Van Halen drama, Sammy issued a dizzying array of albums under his own name and with a number of bands—Waboritas, Chickenfoot, The Circle—and toured heavily, playing these songs plus Montrose and Van Halen chestnuts. Nothing's certified except the first Chickenfoot (at gold), given the promotion and excitement back in 2009 of the supergroup act, which consisted of Sammy, Michael, Joe Satriani, and Chad Smith from The Red Hot Chili Peppers.

Depending on how you count, it's about twenty-five albums, but in some respects, the records in the 2000s are more so an excuse to party, given Sammy's success at branding himself as Mr. Cabo Wabo, a sort of hard rock Jimmy Buffett. In fact, Sammy's most successful solo act has been the selling of 80 percent of his Cabo Wabo tequila business to the Italian Gruppo Campari group for $80 million.

No such windfall for Diamond Dave, although he's had his run of success, too. Unlike Sammy, who made eleven albums before he arrived in Van Halen, Dave saw the release of his first solo album in 1986 after leaving the band. His *Crazy from the Heat* EP had already gone platinum by the time *Eat 'Em and Smile* emerged. That would go platinum quickly, with the *Skyscraper* follow-up certifying at that level, too, although not until 2012. The solid *A Little Ain't Enough* album from 1991, featuring Jason Becker on guitar, would go gold.

But then that would be the end for Dave, whose eccentric personality could not be contained across three Van Halen–adjacent records. First, he tried an album of myriad rock and non-rock styles called *Your Filthy Little Mouth*, which was a critical and sales disaster. Next came a return to something akin to *A Little Ain't Enough*, in 1998's dumbly monikered *DLR Band*. Issued on Wawazat!! Records, the creditable heavy rockin' Bob Marlette/John 5 joint sunk without a trace. From there, things just got more Dave, in fact, *Diamond Dave*. That was the name of his mostly covers album on prog rock imprint Magna Carta. One supposes the idea was to do a full-length version of *Crazy from the Heat*, but nobody was buyin', with the album suffering the same "Here today, gone later today" fate as *DLR Band*.

To chuck Gary Cherone into the mix, amusingly, he's seen about the same level of success as Dave and Sammy, although the solo dimension is a mere footnote. His claim to fame is Extreme, with the band's second album, *Pornograffitti*, going double-platinum and follow-up, *III Sides to Every Story*, selling gold. There was another one in 1995, again in 2008, and later up into 2023. He's also got a solo EP, an album as Tribe of Judah, and two with a side project called Hurtsmile.

To close, let's go back to the premise that Dave and Sammy did about as good as each other. To adjust that, we'd have to give the edge—more than an edge—to Sammy, because creativity and legacy count. Although he's not got a revered classic anywhere in those twenty-five albums like *Montrose* (and yes, every Van Halen would be lesser), he's made a bunch of great music and, more importantly, thrown hundreds of boozy, fun-in-the-sun parties over the decades, with an uncommon amount of those shows literally in the sun. And yet we'd have to admit that the couple years of mania around Dave from the summer of 1986 through to the end of 1988 would be more intense than Sammy ever saw as a solo artist across fully fifty years in the biz.

And then here comes Gary, with the only double-platinum album between all of them! Again, what's interesting is what this tells us about career and fame, how each of these cats can live such different rock 'n' roll lives yet all somehow wind up with the same sort of peak of success and, on top of that, for about the same couple of years' duration.

A jump to Geffen in 1982 sent Sammy platinum with *Standing Hampton* and *VOA*, and gold with *Three Lock Box*.

SAMMY HAGAR

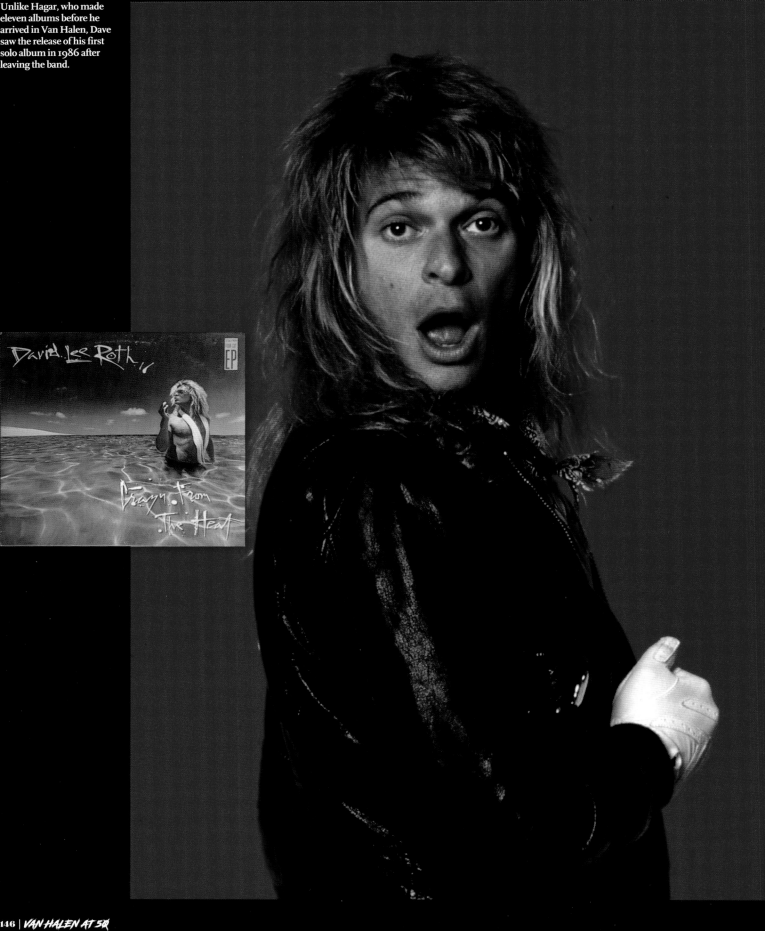

Unlike Hagar, who made eleven albums before he arrived in Van Halen, Dave saw the release of his first solo album in 1986 after leaving the band.

Gary doesn't care what the author thinks of Van Halen *III*. Here he is performing with Extreme at Empire Rockfest in Belleville, Ontario, July 26, 2014.

41

BEATS WORKIN'

THE SECOND COMPILATION:
THE BEST OF BOTH WORLDS

THE BEST OF BOTH WORLDS
VAN HALEN

First stop of the Van Halen reunion tour, Greensboro, North Carolina, June 11, 2004

Something I think we can appreciate about the Van Halen camp is that they weren't gratuitous with compilations and live albums. *The Best of Both Worlds*, issued July 20, 2004, is only the band's second hits pack, and it was to be the last. The release coincided with the Red Rocker rejoining the band, although no new studio album was managed.

Still, the guys did one better than the two new David Lee Roth songs on *Best of Volume I* and put together three new songs with Sammy, which kick off this two-CD set, right after dedicating the first track to "Eruption," which is actually a pretty cool idea. Unfortunately, Michael hadn't rejoined the band when the new songs were recorded, so Eddie plays the bass on them, even if they did manage to get Michael in to provide backing vocals.

Package-wise, the two CDs (featuring remastered versions of the songs) came housed in a fat digipak featuring Eddie's iconic, zigzagged, red, black, and white guitar pattern, accented with spot varnish. Inside were artful black-and-white shots of the band (with Sammy only), a discography with thumbnail album cover shots, and a liner essay from *Rolling Stone*'s David Wild.

Back to the trio of new songs, arguably what we have here is the loudest, proudest presentation of Van Halen's brown sound ever barely caged to tape. Casual as they are at the riff end and with regard to the lyrics, the playing is red-hot and the production positively earthquaking, as is evidenced by the brutish bluster of smoke-choked Eddie we hear at the very onset of the first song, "It's About Time." And "Up for Breakfast" is as joyous of groove as anything in the catalog, with Alex on drums and Eddie on bass and guitar stretching time and then snapping it back, dialed in crushing, with an ageless Sammy screaming powerfully up top. "Learning to See" is a little more reflective, with Sammy's musings placed over an amusing, noisy power ballad structure, again, like the other songs, stretched and swooped and loose.

Across all three, the guys seem to be challenging themselves to create songs from jams through the sheer force of undeniable chemistry. And in the booking of the studio and the cooking of the songs, they break as many rules as might have been breached back at *Women and Children First*. Predictably, none of the new songs did much at the box office, but the album certified as platinum in the United States, reaching an impressive #3 spot on the Billboard 200, while finding #2 in Canada and #15 in the United Kingdom, where it also earned a gold award.

The balance of the thirty-six-track album was split pretty much evenly between the Dave and the Sammy eras, with one wild card being three tracks from the *Live: Right Here, Right Now.* album. There's no representation from the *III* album with Gary Cherone. After all, if there had been, they'd have to come up with a new album title, wouldn't they?

42

WHEN IT'S LOVE

"DIMEBAG" DARRELL BURIED WITH ONE OF EDDIE'S PRIZED GUITARS

Pantera's Abbott Brothers Vinnie and "Dimebag" Darrell had been making a valiant go of it with their new band Damageplan—I'd interviewed Vinnie in January 2004 and met up with both of them in Toronto in June—but were playing the clubs. Not that it mattered to Dime, who just wanted to wail away on his guitar and meet the fans. Three months later Dime was meeting the Van Halen guys for the first time—Vinnie had already partied with Eddie at the band's strip club a few days earlier—drinking with them before and after the Van Halen show in Lubbock, Texas, September 29, arriving on a limo sent by the band.

A month later, December 8 at the Alrosa Villa in Columbus, Ohio, the brothers had just said their customary last words before hitting the stage. "Van Halen" was a shared invocation to be loose and have fun but also to be musical and creative. Dime's biggest inspiration had been Eddie, and it had served him well, with the mighty Pantera ruling the entirety of the '90s as the coolest, most dangerous heavy metal band on the planet, with Dime constantly showing up in the guitar magazines as the most beloved textbook guitar hero of the era besides a still well-regarded Eddie Van Halen. Moments into the Damageplan set, a crazed gunman appeared onstage, killing Dime with five bullets to the head. Three others died as well before the gunman was killed by police.

Dime and his longtime partner Rita had been in communication with Eddie to buy one of Eddie's iconic striped guitars, with Eddie in turn telling him he'd do one better and make him one personally. When Rita was asked if it was red, black, and white that he preferred, she said no, because Darrell had always said that the black-and-yellow "bumblebee" Charvel hybrid Eddie is sporting on the back cover of Van Halen II was his favorite, calling it Eddie's "toughest" guitar.

A week after the massacre in Ohio, at Dime's funeral on December 14 in Arlington, Texas, Eddie showed up along with Dime's guitar, only it wasn't a new build. As Eddie said at the service, "Dime was an original and only an original deserves the original." Eddie was too broken up to enter the room where Dime had laid in state (in a Kiss Kasket donated by Gene Simmons), with Rita and Damageplan tech John Graham taking the famous guitar and placing it in the casket. Rita, with a kiss to Dime's forehead, said, "See baby, you didn't get a replica; you got the one."

Attending Dime's funeral along with Eddie were Jerry Cantrell, Corey Taylor, Dino Cazares from Fear Factory, and Zakk Wylde, with whom Eddie shared numerous shots. Eddie, typically quite shy, rose to the occasion and spoke, saying, "I'm here for the same reason as everyone else, to give some love back. This guy was full of life. He lived and breathed rock 'n' roll." Eddie also held his cell phone up to the mic. "Thank you so much, man," we heard from Dime, in response to his experience in Lubbock, "for the most awesome, uplifting, euphoric, spiritual rock 'n' roll extravaganza ever." As brother Vinnie recalled, on the plane back after the Van Halen concert, Darrell had turned to him and said, "Man, if this plane crashed and I died tonight, I would be okay with it because we got to meet Van Halen."

The legendary Dimebag
Darrell, delivering the
goods on the *Cowboys from
Hell* tour

43

BEST OF BOTH WORLDS

DAVE APPEARS ON BLUEGRASS VAN HALEN COVERS ALBUM

Following up on similar tributes to Radiohead and Metallica, on June 6, 2006, CMH Records issued an album called *Strummin' with the Devil: The Southern Side of Van Halen*. In what world is this a Van Halen career milestone? Well, it really isn't, but it's indicative of the surrealism David Lee Roth brought to the band, because there he is, performing on two tracks and going on TV and doing interviews about the project.

In other words, he's doing the band a service by keeping it in the news while also carrying on the tradition of having fun with the brand. He's reminding us of Van Halen's roots in traditional music and also drawing a bead to Van Halen songs like "Ice Cream Man," "Big Bad Bill (Is Sweet William Now)," "Could This Be Magic?," and even, at a stretch, "Take Your Whiskey Home," "The Full Bug," and "Spanish Fly." But yes, on a more abstract level, it's Dave demonstrating that in Van Halen World, anything might happen. There might be a tour with Sammy Hagar, or Dave might go back to school to train as an EMT, after which he'd sign on for night shift duties in his newly adopted home of New York City. He might assemble some drinking buddies and explore the Amazon or climb a mountain, or he might become a very high-profile (but ill-fated and short-lived) radio host. Or, in this case, Dave might walk into the room and sing on a couple of bluegrass renditions of Van Halen songs—namely, "Jamie's Cryin'" and "Jump"— fronting The John Jorgenson Bluegrass Band, with the legendary Jorgenson also serving as the producer of the project.

In support of the record (which managed a #66 placement on the Billboard Top Country Albums chart), Dave appeared on a number of high-profile TV shows, including Fox News and *The View*, where he charmed the crowd with a nice, clean interview and performed "Jump" with a seven-piece band (of note, everybody in the crowd got a copy of the album). Closing Jay Leno's late-night show, he performed with the same band, consisting of fiddle,

banjo, mandolin, stand-up bass, and three guys with acoustic guitars, one laid flat and getting some slide action. Dave strode center stage, short hair, yellow shirt, and jeans and did a bang-up job with the band's thoughtful arrangement, replete with different chords and a false ending.

On *Conan*, July 13, Dave and a six-piece configuration did their laid-back, country version of "Jamie's Cryin'." Once more, Dave turned on the charm, singing abundantly and accurately, in front of a band of players turning in thoughtful parts, weaving rhythm and licks and solo spots expertly. In tandem, however, Dave was keeping the engine running by touring with his solo band, playing most of the summer of '06 and into the fall. It would place him in good stead for something he told the women from *The View* was inevitable: a reunion with Van Halen. After all, he quipped,

"What's more American than Van Halen in the summertime? Sooner than later, all the planets will merge for the brothers, and we'll be right back on your show."

44
JUDGMENT DAY

VAN HALEN INDUCTED INTO ROCK & ROLL HALL OF FAME

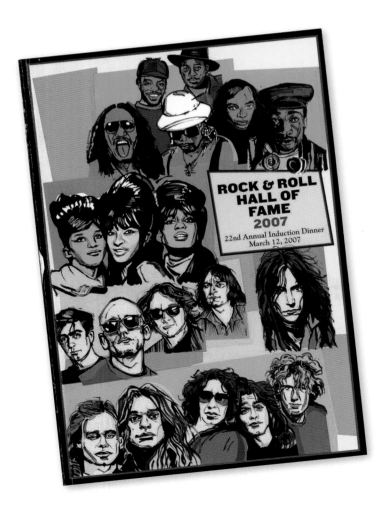

Van Halen's long-anticipated induction into the Rock & Roll Hall of Fame, taking place March 12, 2007, in New York City, arguably couldn't have gone much worse. Inductors and bad apples Velvet Revolver were doomed from the start, having the previous year been asked to induct The Sex Pistols, which went down like a lead balloon even worse than this year's try. Their collective speech seemed forced and insincere, each guy delivering his lame pre-written line like a bad comic hungover and not trying to be funny.

But, fair enough, rock stars aren't always the best at giving speeches. Come performance time, Slash kicked things off by flubbing the intro riff to "Ain't Talkin' 'bout Love," after which the band rallied. Then Scott Weiland started singing, and things got weird again. Not only was he straightening out the vocal melody, but he sang the song in an odd sort of lower-register Louis Armstrong voice, lots of growl and vocal fry. It's almost as if he was making fun of David Lee Roth, presenting a caricature of a specific, showbiz-y component of Dave's style. Crazy and pretty cool Iggy Pop dancing, though. Then came what was ostensibly a nod to Van Hagar with "Runaround." It's an obscure choice to be sure, but then again, Velvet Revolver didn't bother to learn it, instead turning in a sort of punk rock version of something that resembled the chorus, essentially an outro jam with Weiland yelling "round and round" over and over again.

As for the band's acceptance, well, Eddie had just gone into rehab, so he wasn't there. Alex stayed away in solidarity with his brother. Dave, on the other hand, got into a dispute with Velvet Revolver about song choice, so that served as any number of excuses for him not to show. As Sammy framed it, Dave wanted to hog both songs. As Weiland put it, there was no way Velvet Revolver was going to play "Jump." Gary Cherone wasn't invited, so that was a moot point. Gary said that, although he was a small part of the band's history, he was not part of their legend.

That left Sammy Hagar and Michael Anthony to pick up the pieces. In other words, less than half the relevant band was there, with Sammy even letting it be known in interviews around the event that it wasn't a slam-dunk that even *he'd* be allowed to be part of the official induction. But having got the nod, he said that even a shotgun couldn't keep him way, with Sammy sincerely expressing gratitude to the Hall for having him, and then thanking a long list of people, considerately.

As for further positives, Sammy and Michael performed a groovy, spirited version of "Why Can't This Be Love" with the house band, and Michael's speech, like Sammy's, was heartfelt and respectful, with Michael thanking Warner Bros., Ed Leffler, his parents, his wife and daughters, and even his sister, who turned him on to rock 'n' roll with a Blue Cheer album (very likely *Vincebus Eruptum*). He also made sure to thank Gary, "because you were part of this too, man." Concerning Eddie's absence, he said that Eddie's "home getting some help," with Sammy adding that, "I think Eddie's gonna come out the other side a better person and maybe we'll get our buddy back."

Joined at the hip. Sammy and Mikey at the Rock & Roll Hall of Fame induction ceremonies at the Waldorf Astoria in New York City, March 12, 2007

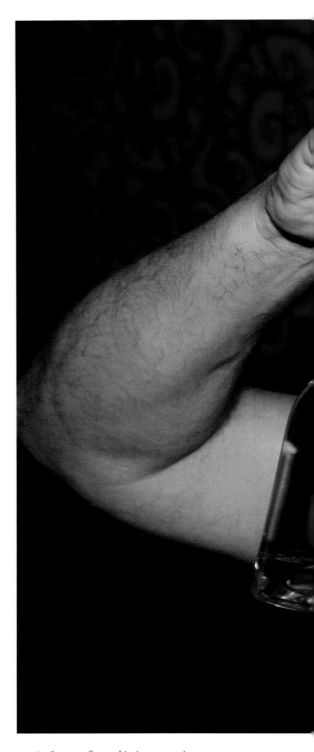

45

HOW MANY SAY I

SAMMY SELLS MAJORITY OF HIS TEQUILA BUSINESS

Here's one that most fans would agree is part of the Van Halen story, even though it's seemingly a couple steps removed. On May 7, 2007, Sammy announces that he's selling 80 percent of his tequila business to Italy's Gruppo Campari for $8 million, with subsidiary Skyy Spirits out of San Francisco to do the marketing.

That is key, because growing the business had become too hot to handle for Sammy, who, after all, wanted to be a rock star, too. Sammy's Cabo Wabo tequila brand had begun life in 1996 as a private house brand tequila manufactured by a family-owned producer nearby his infamous party joint of the same name in Cabo San Lucas, Mexico, which he had opened way back in April 1990. Venturing into the States with it, he had hoped to sell 10,000 cases of the elixir, but instead, through the hard work of a wine importer from his native Napa Valley, he'd moved 37,000 in his first year, rising to 147,000 in 2006. The awards were piling up as well, helping turn Cabo Wabo into the second best-selling premium tequila in the United States. "Mas Tequila," indeed.

As Sammy framed it, it was getting embarrassing fielding calls (on his cell phone, on the beach!) from "friends" who lamented not being able to get Cabo Wabo in all sorts of different countries around the world. Admitting to not being much of a day-to-day business guy, the deal was struck to bring on partners, in the form of the sixth biggest booze company in the world. As Sammy would chuckle, this was more money than he'd ever made in twenty years playing with one of the biggest (and best) bands in the world.

Up into July 2010, Campari exercised an option from the original deal and purchased the remaining 20 percent, netting Sammy an additional $11 million. That's less of a haul proportionally, given that sales of premium spirits had sagged with the economic crash of 2008/2009, with Cabo Wabo selling about fifty-six thousand cases in 2009, down 12.5 percent from the previous year. Still, the whole point was to get the brand worldwide, and as Sammy chuckled at the time, "They don't want me to change anything. They said, 'We love what you've done with this company; that's why we wanted you involved. If anything, get another tattoo.'"

Since then, Sammy's stayed an enthusiastic ambassador for the brand, while also launching Sammy's Beach Bar Rum in 2011 and, in partnership with Maroon 5's Adam Levine, Santo Mezquila (a mescal and tequila blend) in 2017. In 2020, Sammy's buddy Rick Springfield joined him in the rum business, and now, spiked by the rum, there are also Sammy's Beach Bar Cocktails. Up into 2022, in time for his seventy-fifth birthday, Sammy announced the sale of a special-edition, five-hundred-bottle run of his rum called Sammy's Lost Cask. Although production of his pirate's booze had since been relocated to Puerto Rico, this was a run of the rum that had been discovered "rested in paradise" back in Makawao, Maui, Hawaii, where Sammy had originally started the offshoot business.

46

FINISH WHAT YA STARTED

BAND REUNITES WITH DAVE AND HITS THE ROAD

After so many fits and starts they wanted to be sure, and so the announcement of a new Van Halen tour fronted by David Lee Roth came on August 13, 2007, just six weeks before the first date, on September 27, in Charlotte, North Carolina. Raining on the parade would be the news that Michael Anthony wouldn't be playing bass, replaced rather by Eddie's sixteen-year-old son, Wolfgang. Putting a wide-smiled positive spin on it, Dave said that Wolfgang added a certain youthful enthusiasm to the show and that Van Halen felt like "a new band."

The tour began as 2007 dates only, but they were selling out everywhere, prompting an extension into 2008, notwithstanding a series of postponed dates in March and early April and some cancellations later on. As it played out, the band performed essentially all of October, November, and December 2007. As for 2008, a second leg went from January 22 to February 20, followed by a last run from April 17 through June 2—these were mostly makeup dates, but even here, we saw some cancellations—with an outlier festival date in Quebec City, Quebec, on July 3. The campaign, seventy-six shows in total, was eventually rechristened the Van Halen 2007–2008 North American tour, and yes, in the main it was an American affair, with a half-dozen Canadian shows and none outside of those two countries. Support

through February 20, 2008, was Bob Marley's son Ky-Mani Marley and then, after that through to the end, neo-soul singer Ryan Shaw. In other words, Van Halen continued their long-standing tradition of being creative and unexpected with their support billing choices.

As for the reviews, by all accounts fans and critics were super-pleased (the author caught the Toronto show on October 7, 2007), bowdlerization of the classic lineup notwithstanding. Dave had put together a look befitting his advanced age, with sober dress shirts and slacks, often all black, and for rare flash, a matador's jacket. His hair was cut short, as was Eddie's, Alex's, and Wolfgang's. Eddie and his son also dressed pretty darned casual, with the flashiest thing onstage being Alex's massive kit, replete with gong, and the artful S-shaped staging. At the performance end, Wolfgang turned out to be a powerhouse, shoulder to shoulder as one of the top three musicians onstage. And the singing? Dave was being Dave, conversational, compromising the melodies, as much acting out the songs as he was singing them.

The true star was the set list, a welcome change from the Sammy-era running order that was emphatically, through the insistence of the front man, conspicuously lacking in Dave-era classics. Revenge was sweet, because now there were no Sammy songs at all, turning Van Halen Mk IV into a racing car. Ergo, there goes the likes of "I'm the One," "Romeo Delight," "Somebody Get Me a Doctor," "Atomic Punk," "Everybody Wants Some!!," "Mean Street," "Unchained," "And the Cradle Will Rock . . . ," "Hot for Teacher," and "Panama," turning the show into a shoot-'em-up fest of Van Halen at their heaviest. At a $93 million gross, the campaign was framed as Van Halen's most successful tour ever, proving that, despite the growing piles of dirty laundry, fans were willing to push them aside and party.

Gwinnett Center Arena, Duluth, Georgia, May 11, 2008

47
BLACK AND BLUE

A DIFFERENT KIND OF TRUTH:
THE SHOCKING LAST ALBUM

It's important and central to the baking, but people make too much of the fact that *A Different Kind of Truth* features a bunch of Van Halen songs as old as the mid-1970s reworked. Fact is, Van Halen poked around in the vaults for most of the albums they've made. To be sure, as Dave put it at the time, this one is much more so "a collaboration with the past," but still, the old songs repurposed are quite overhauled musically, with Wolfgang fancying up all the bass lines and Dave rewriting the lyrics to be more autobiographical of his life in 2011. What's more, there are a bunch of new compositions, too; and everything is performed anew by the modern-day version of these three guys (plus one new guy) and produced anew by the quietly respected John Shanks, recommended for the job by Dave.

The end result, issued February 7, 2012, surprised everyone with its heaviness, its fierceness, and its guitar madness, with the only keyboards on the album being incidental synthesizer by Dave on advance single "Tattoo." To be sure, a few of the songs sound dated at the riff end of things, like a band writing hard rock in 1976, and Dave's lyrics can be over-the-top with bumper sticker bon mots. But those are minor quibbles on a record that is defiantly dirty and anti-commercial and often frantic.

Wolfgang, a big part of the writing, the production, and joyous, intrusive Billy Sheehan–like bass inventiveness, rues that new song, and album-opener "Tattoo" was picked as the lead single. The amusing part is that we all thought it sounded pretty heavy for a first single—that is, until we heard the whole thing and it took its place as one of the poppiest things on an otherwise aggressive, relentless record.

Next is "She's the Woman," based on "Voodoo Queen" from 1976. This one's classic high-quality old Van Halen all the way, with a sort of *II* vibe, steely of riff, funky and grinding of rhythm, but again a little wisecracking at the lyric end. "You and Your Blues" is all new but with a surprise nod to "One I Want" from the Gary Cherone album. Speed metal monster "China Town" is also all new—that's Wolfie tapping on bass at the beginning, with a capo turning his performance piccolo. "Blood and Fire" is mostly new, built on a riff that goes back to a piece of music of Eddie's from 1984 called "Ripley."

Come "Bullethead" and we're back to the ferocious mighty metal of "China Town," with Wolfgang describing the song as "straight-up punk." Of course, with Dad writing the riff, it's much more than that, even if Dave makes us think punk, given his occasionally herky-jerky vocal phrasing. Strength to strength, the sense of electrocuted axe-mad distortion established thus far is maintained with the likes of "As Is" and "Honeybabysweetiedoll," both new and both heavy and nutty with Dave rising to the challenge, again in hysterics, incredulous as the fireworks factory blows up around him.

Here at the heart of the album, you really begin to settle into the fact that there's a lot of razor's edge playing from Eddie, as well as new effects getting used, with Eddie no doubt inspired by his son's busy performance and also Wolfie's enthusiastic and studious traffic-directing of these old ideas, twisting them, editing and curating the album. Here at the dark heart of this curiously titled record, what Eddie said about the album being made purely for the enjoyment of himself and the band really rings true. Fortunately, it's what the long-time fans—and fans of Eddie as noisemaker—would have wanted, not that we had any realistic reason to ask for it, much less any kind of Van Halen album at all at this point!

"The Trouble with Never" and "Outta Space" (previously "Let's Get Rockin'") demonstrate further heaviness and riffiness but also the chemistry of Alex and Wolfgang as a rhythm section, captured hot by Shanks' sizzling production job. "Stay Frosty" is essentially "Ice Cream Man" part two, complete with Dave on acoustic guitar at the start. The album's final two tracks, "Big River" and "Beats Workin'," bring us full circle to my earlier thought: that some of this album really does sound like it's 1974, although thankfully very little of it. But yes, these two are as close as we get to "Little Dreamer" and "Feel Your Love Tonight"—namely, sort of bar band rock best left in the vaults as developmental curios.

Still, despite the droop at the end (of an admirable fifty-minute presentation), *A Different Kind of Truth* is a bombshell way for Van Halen to sign off. In fact, completely unexpectedly given the big business significance of the Van Halen band and brand, this remains the best and coolest example of a heritage act late in the game surprising its base with old-school heavy metal fireworks anywhere in the rock 'n' roll history books. In that sense, forget about Wolfie calling "Bullethead" punk rock; the whole album—and by extension Van Halen at this point—is punk rock, with Eddie putting art (or at least the art of blazing, shredding guitar) above commerciality and then Dave putting his own kind of punk stamp on it as well, singing (and talking) over and over again about independence and taking risks.

It's no surprise that *A Different Kind of Truth* hit #2 on the Billboard charts and sold briskly despite precipitous declines in physical CD sales by this point. By the end of 2012, it had gotten to 411,000 copies and surely not long after would have gone gold. Why no one has revisited the numbers and got that done is anybody's guess, because *A Different Kind of Truth* currently sits as the only Van Halen studio album not certified at the gold level or higher. Then again, that's what a punk rock band would do.

Promoting *A Different Kind of Truth* at the US Airways Center in Phoenix, June 16, 2012. Opening on the campaign was Kool & the Gang.

A DIFFERENT KIND OF TRUTH II: A PROPOSED NEXT VAN HALEN ALBUM

Call this a list of the twelve greatest Van Halen rarities if you like, but it's a little more than that. We all know that *A Different Kind of Truth* is an album of many previously non-LP Van Halen songs reimagined and rerecorded. Well, here's a batch of more golden Van Halen nuggets, sequenced into a follow-up album. In this case, however, I envision Wolfgang cleaning them up, "joining" the band as second guitarist (and/or bassist), and adding to what's there. Or maybe for the worst of it just rescue the vocal—or better yet, get Dave in and redo some of them. Plus, of course, he's the producer.

Consider the rarity "One More Time" a slightly more leaden version of ZZ Top's "Beer Drinkers and Hell Raisers." Eddie with Billy F Gibbons, backstage at the LA Forum, March 1982.

1. "EYES OF THE NIGHT"

We kick off the album with this fast, technical enough rocker, recorded live at the Whisky on May 29, 1976. "Eyes of the Night" features smart chord changes and novel battering ram percussion. There's even modulation, sweet backup vocals, and a few inversions of time signature. All told, there's more than enough firepower and weirdness and action points to bode well for the album. As for the lyrics? It's a love song . . . through binoculars.

2. "BAD WOMEN"

This one wouldn't need much work, because it was part of the 1977 Warner Bros. demos. It's bright, it's bold, the beat is perfect, and everybody performs well. As for the structure, it's at the slow end of mid-paced, with a novel riff of stacked chords rife with pregnant pauses. The bonus comes with the dramatic ascending chords at the solo section.

3. "HERE'S JUST WHAT YOU WANTED"

Pretty incredible that this California bar band was constructing galloping New Wave of British Heavy Metal-type (NWOBHM) anthems three years before that hallowed explosion of hard rock emerged. The verse chords are dark and European, but the chorus warms it up a bit, with nice harmonies and hook line. This one could've held its own on *Narita* or *Fire Down Under* by Riot.

4. "I WANT SOME ACTION"

Raucous but bizarre, "I Want Some Action" hails from the *5150* sessions and is easily top third against the rest of that album. There's a tinge of the blues to it, but it's mostly a kind of late '70s/early '80s stomping heavy metal, maybe something that could have fit on ZZ Top's *Eliminator* with a whole different production approach. Wolfie is going to have to figure out how to wipe Sammy's vocal and either get Dave to sing this one or do it himself.

5. "ONE MORE TIME"

Here's a snarling mid-paced number, mean of riff, like hard-charged hair metal from 1983. Consider it a slightly more leaden version of ZZ Top's "Beer Drinkers and Hell Raisers," a little boogie-woogie when Dave is singing but gnarly in between his wise couplets. It's never been recorded as a demo; however, you can hear it live from October of '77.

6. "BELIEVE ME"

Eddie turns in a ferocious, interesting riff for this smart, percussive rocker, percussive because Alex is forced to follow Eddie wherever he goes. You can hear a number of versions of this song from as far back as 1974, but the best is from a soundboard recording captured by Mike Kelley, January 18, 1977, at the Starwood.

7. "YOUNG & WILD"

From the 1977 demo, "Young & Wild" is a song penned by Kim Fowley and Stephen Tetsch, but Van Halen make it their own, most notably with the strong harmony vocals. It provides another tempo and rhythm to our imagined album, being pretty close to a fully thumping four-on-the-floor. The Runaways (managed by Fowley) recorded it for one of their albums. Also of note, Tetsch is none other than Venus, of Venus and the Razorblades, whom Van Halen had supported.

8. "WOMAN IN LOVE"

Here's a groovy, funky party rocker with an irresistible riff imaginable as an Aerosmith, Blackfoot, or ZZ Top song (I'm hearing a bit of "Francine" here). It provides light relief on our fantasy album, not quite "Ice Cream Man" but maybe serving the purpose of "Beautiful Girls." An excellent live recording exists from June 18, 1975. By the way, it's got nothing to do with "Women in Love" from Van Halen *II*.

9. "GLITTER"

This one goes back to the 1973 demo, and yet it really doesn't sound particularly old. Okay, well, maybe there's a little Captain Beyond or Sir Lord Baltimore to it, but Eddie's really at the front edge of his riff writing here. Unfortunately, the solo section is placed on a sort of basic Black Sabbath downer rock chord sequence. Still, it provides some variety to our imagined album, especially since there are no ballads!

10. "I WANNA BE YOUR LOVER"

Eddie turns in a molten funk metal riff here, with Alex and Michael responding in kind with a busy, groovy rhythmic performance. Glorious on the 1977 demo, I would have liked to have seen this on the debut instead of "Little Dreamer" or "Feel Your Love Tonight"—it's in that orbit but with more swagger.

11. "NO MORE WAITING"

Another thumping rocker in a mid-paced zone, featuring interesting vocal phrasing over a sort of blustery, bluesy, funky heavy metal chord sequence. You can hear live versions of this from 1977 and even 1978. Alternately called "Get Off My Back" and "Show No Mercy."

12. "WE DIE BOLD"

We're back to another sort of NWOBHM rocker here, in terms of "We Die Bold" (also called "We Die Young") being a sort of cross between a gallop and an up-tempo shuffle but with epic European chord changes. Michael is rock-solid on the simple, driving bass line, helping make this song a fortified castle rocker.

48
JUMP
VAN HALEN ISSUE
TOKYO DOME
LIVE IN CONCERT

There seemed to be a bit of a pattern in later years with Van Halen making odd business decisions, although sometimes for the better, point being the barnstormer of an album we got out of the guys as their final salvo. But come time for a follow-up to *A Different Kind of Truth*, they considered an album of their demos cleaned up but couldn't find the tapes, although YouTube posters seem to have been able. Van Halen also thought about putting out an archival live compilation built from bootlegs capturing shows from the club days—interesting but somewhat undermining of the process that gave us *A Different Kind of Truth*.

Instead, they went with a conventional live album, although the care that resulted in Alex approving only a single live album thus far—and laboriously doctored at that—well, that sober procedure went out the window. At least they had 150 shows since 2007 to choose from, with those tapes given the fighting chance by having ProTools rigged up right at the mixing board each night, at least during the present tour. But then they decided not to do any touch-ups at all. Against their usual 5150 mad lab tendencies, they'd just let it all hang

out as raw as it was on any given night, plus allow Dave to pick the show, just to keep the peace.

Dave went with June 21, 2013, at the Tokyo Dome in Tokyo, Japan, from what was essentially an isolated spate of dates after the 2012 *A Different Kind of Truth* tour proper, which had been conducted the previous spring. Dave had an affinity for Japan and even kept a place there. What's more, he was learning the language, as was evidenced by his raps on the two-CD album, issued March 31, 2015. Hard to believe that Dave, given his usual touchiness about his reputation, couldn't see that his vocals were less than optimal, although as one settles in for the duration, it's not the debacle chirped about at the time. In fact, protests were so loud that a conspiracy grew that the Van Halen brothers let the album come out that way just to humiliate Dave.

Molson Canadian Amphitheatre, Toronto, August 7, 2015

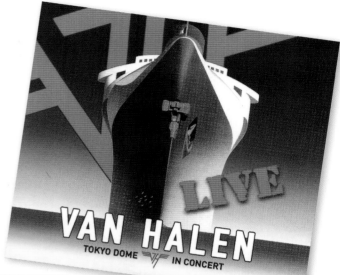

Van Halen performs on Hollywood Boulevard in Los Angeles for *Jimmy Kimmel Live!*, March 30, 2015.

PNC Bank Arts Center,
Holmdel, New Jersey,
August 9, 2015

So, what's the problem? Well, unfortunately, one could argue that the worst performance from Dave is on "Unchained," and darn it if that isn't the first track of fully twenty-three on the album. And now a pattern is established: You're constantly distracted listening for flubs, one minute cheering him on, rationalizing what he's doing, praising his comedic skills and then consoling yourself that all is well when Eddie and his son come to the rescue with sweet and accurate backing vocals. But the next minute it's back to wrinkling your nose at the dropped and changed words, the bad vocal phrasing, the herky-jerky timing, and the more than occasional flatness and sharpness, aggravatingly heard in a yelp just as often as part of a lyric.

And that's the crazy thing—although Dave's world is regularly crazy, so what do you expect? Take album closer "Jump," for instance. Dave sings it with a renewed, ill-considered, and, most annoyingly, higher and more challenging vocal melody than he needs to. It would have been easier to sing it like it's *1984* all over again, and yet the showman in him can't be contained. One supposes that's the magic of David Lee Roth—he's being dangerous up there, he's being loose, he's trying things out, living in the moment. But again, to reiterate, the bottom line is, you come away with the attitude that Diamond Dave can still sing; it's just that he often chooses not to. Why? Who knows? Maybe it's *he*

that is spiting the band, turning the tables, playing 3D chess. Or maybe he's trying to teach the Van Halen fans that rock 'n' roll is best lived on the edge.

Furthermore, we've often talked about how the album cover art and even the title of the album is a hasty and ill-conceived botch. But putting these quibbles aside, Van Halen fans can indeed sun themselves to a crisp as they celebrate finally getting a live album with Dave on it. And not only that, *Tokyo Dome* is fired by the flamethrower love of *A Different Kind of Truth*, with the band blazing and the production job balancing noise with power. What's more, given the circumstances, we get fully three songs from the current album—namely, "She's the Woman," "Tattoo," and a lurching, violent "China Town." Elsewhere, gems we thought we'd never hear abound, with *Tokyo Dome* bestowing upon us the likes of "I'll Wait," "I'm the One," "Hear About It Later," "Romeo Delight," and "Beautiful Girls."

Again, we've half-joked about Van Halen going punk rock on us, but that sense of defiance at industry norms (and at the band's own place in the machine), along with belief in spontaneous performance, is very much part and parcel of this hot blast of Diamond Dave at last. With the shock Mohawk of the studio album making a statement, *Tokyo Dome* winds up serving as the exclamation point. Such frenzied activity couldn't possibly last, but no one anticipated the ultimate and tragic reason why.

49
JAMIE'S CRYIN'
VAN HALEN TOUR FOR THE LAST TIME

As the Van Halen ocean liner crashed through the frothy seas of 2015, it looked like Van Halen had got their business sorted. Eddie looked happier and healthier than he had in years, although the same couldn't be said for Wolfgang, who seemed to be getting heavier and heavier. But a tour was planned, nicely timed to support a double live album. What's more, the band was going to do live TV, also perfectly timed to promote *Tokyo Dome*. First came a short concert on *Jimmy Kimmel Live*, March 30 and 31, with the band appearing again a couple days later on *The Ellen DeGeneres Show*.

For *Kimmel*, Dave was sporting a bandage on his nose, having cracked it with a mic stand. Clad in a frumpy jeans and jean jacket getup and no shirt, he proceeded to put on a typical late-period Dave show, above average as a front man in terms of keeping the party going but, as usual, demonstrating only a casual relationship with the nub of the job at hand. Come time for Ellen, and Dave had slipped right off the page, butchering "Dance the Night Away" but rallying a bit for "Jump."

The Pavilion, Concord, California, July 9, 2015

Then it was time for the tour, beginning in Seattle on July 5, 2015, with the band playing pretty much solid through to October 2, where, at the Hollywood Bowl in hometown Los Angeles, Van Halen performed the last concert of their forty-year career. Supporting was southern blues rocker Kenny Wayne Shepherd, again Van Halen making us think as we bought our drinks. But soon it was time for the main event, with the guys continuing to play musicologist by deepening the set list even beyond the thrilling rock rides delivered in 2007, 2008, 2012, and 2013. Highlights included "Light Up the Sky" as bracing slap-to-the-face opener, along with "Romeo Delight" and "Drop Dead Legs" early in the sequence. Later we got "Little Guitars," ""Dirty Movies,"" "Women in Love," and, for a spell, "In a Simple Rhyme." Shows closed with the powerhouse but expected "You Really Got Me," "Panama," and foamy anthem to euphoria, "Jump."

All told, the tour went without a hitch, comprising thirty-nine shows and grossing $26 million. If there was any reason to think it was the end, it wasn't coming from Eddie or Alex or, over to our left, Wolfgang Van Halen, who was a firecracker of youthful infusion, keeping the old-timers honest. If anything, fans were raising eyebrows at what Dave was doing. But again, the funny thing is, the debate wasn't so much whether he could sing anymore. It was more about whether he was disappearing down the rabbit hole of David Lee Roth as a cartoon character. It looked like he was losing his mind, or, if his plumed display was intentioned, like he'd been taking front man instruction from Vince Neil. In other words, it was something that might have been fixed by a stern lecture from management and/or the brothers. As it turns out, what couldn't be fixed was Eddie's health, with his cancer returning just as he seemed to be taking what looked like a bounding and strideful victory lap for the ages.

Two old adversaries in conversation. Bethel Woods Center for the Arts, Bethel, New York, September 6, 2015

This page and opposite:
Bethel Woods, New York,
September 6, 2015—
about a dozen shows
from the end

50
AFTERSHOCK
THE PASSING OF KING EDWARD

General wear and tear from being a hard-partying rock star across decades of guitar greatness might have been at the root of many of Eddie's problems, including his relationships with Valerie and Janie and, arguably, those with Dave and Sammy, although both could be epic-scale problems in their own rights, especially if you're shy and "not good with words," as Eddie would admit, self-deprecatingly but with charm and authenticity.

Very material was the battle with cancer, the need for hip replacement surgery, and in 2012, a painful abdominal affliction known as diverticulitis, which caused postponement of dates scheduled for Japan. What we didn't know is that soon the cancer would return, manifesting as throat cancer in 2011, with Valerie also letting on in 2019 that it had spread to Eddie's lungs. All manner of traditional and nontraditional attempts at treatment couldn't stop the disease, which Eddie called "a cockroach." Fans had suspected something was up, due to the band's activity. It was a stroke that finally took Eddie Van Halen from us at age 65, on October 6, 2020, complicated by the cancer and now pneumonia. At his side, at the Saint John's Health Center in Santa Monica, California, were Valerie, Janie, Wolfgang, and Alex, his tight-knit family, all beloved and with any broken fences mended.

"I can't believe I'm having to write this," posted Wolfgang in a statement, the day of his dad's passing. "But my father, Edward Lodewijk Van Halen, has lost his long and arduous battle with cancer this morning. He was the best father I could ever ask for. Every moment I've shared with him on and off stage was a gift. My heart is broken and I don't think I'll ever fully recover from this loss. I love you so much, Pop." His bandmates were quick to add their own condolences, as were major rock titans around the world who understood how Eddie had changed the game.

"Heart and soul have been shattered into a million pieces," wrote Janie Van Halen. "I never knew it was possible to cry so many tears or feel such incredible sadness." Valerie Bertinelli reflected that "[t]hroughout all your challenging treatments for lung cancer, you kept your gorgeous spirit and that impish grin. I'm so grateful Wolfie and I were able to hold you in your last moments. I will see you in our next life, my love."

Perhaps Gary Cherone said it best, when he called Eddie a "kind and gentle soul." Over the years, quietly, we'd seen his generosity with Frank and Dweezil Zappa and with "Dimebag" Darrell Abbott, along with his unflagging dedication to his son. Even the eccentric choosing of support bands on Van Halen's mega-exposure tours felt like a show of generosity emanating from the brothers, and in reality, given what we know of his passion for music, the guitarist of the two. Also quietly, in 2017, Eddie pledged his support for music education in school, donating to The Mr. Holland's Opus Foundation seventy-five of his guitars.

But again, Eddie's biggest gift was his music. And really, he died from it. He had the curse of the artist, the torment of the muse, most demonstrative by how much of a gearhead he was and how much time he spent holed up in 5150 rather than how many Van Halen songs got written. And digging in, when we'd complain that some of the songs we officially got were barely written . . . well, that's more a clue that Eddie was the consummate obsessed artist. In effect, or as an abstraction, he was telling us that the creative magic was happening between the notes, marbled around the structured riffs, maybe at the solo spotlight or at the flash-recurring licks. Even more ethereal-like, it lurked in the textures or in the humidity of the chemistry that was so much part of Van Halen's greatness.

In any event, to reiterate, seventy years into rock 'n' roll history, at the apex of the axe position, people talk about Jimi Hendrix and Eddie Van Halen and really no one else. Or when we expand the list, we all know we are talking about mere mortals. In effect, we're all in agreement that as a fount of pure rock 'n' roll creativity, Eddie had been the next and brightest example of the real deal since Jimi, with no one properly substantive in between. And what's beautiful about both those cats, in the end, after all the pyrotechnics, each was shy and soft spoken and self-effacing, genuinely in love with making music and both living and dying for their art. King Edward may no longer be with us, but more than a half-century after "Eruption," his canon of virtuosity—and our memories of that beaming smile on any number of sun-dappled outdoor stages—will always be there to inspire a next generation of artists, be they axe-slingers or otherwise.

The maestro making
beautiful music at
the Rainbow Theatre,
Finsbury Park, London,
October 22, 1978

DISCOGRAPHY

Concerning a few points on format, I've included an additional notes section for anything I thought was interesting, that seemed important. I've left the double quote marks off the song titles here to keep things tidy, although you will see them in the notes section, given that the format there is prosy. I've noted side 1/side 2 designations for all releases from the vinyl era, which I've always maintained ends in 1990. For Van Halen, that would mean *OU812* is our last chunk of vinyl.

Songwriting credits are pretty simple, as Van Halen went with a blanket, full-band credit on everything that wasn't a cover right until the end, barring *A Different Kind of Truth*'s cryptic "VanHalen/Roth" designation, yes, without the space between Van and Halen. As for musician credits, we're not getting into when Eddie plays bass or who exactly is doing backup vocals and so forth. Credits on live albums and compilations are pared back a bit, again, for tidiness. Punctuation and spelling of songs are shown formally as they appear on the earliest releases, but this won't necessarily be maintained elsewhere in the book— for example, this is the only place we'll be showing "Women in Love" with its ridiculous five-dot ellipses.

STUDIO ALBUMS

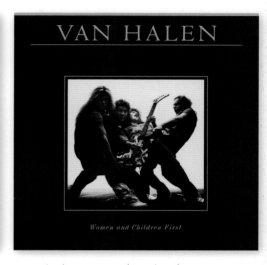

VAN HALEN

Released February 10, 1978; Warner Bros. BSK 3075.

Recorded August 30–September 1977 at Sunset Sound Recorders, Hollywood, CA.

Produced by Ted Templeman.

Side 1: 1. Runnin' with the Devil 3:32; 2. Eruption 1:42; 3. You Really Got Me (Ray Davies) 2:37; 4. Ain't Talkin' 'bout Love 3:47; 5. I'm the One 3:44.

Side 2: 1. Jamie's Cryin' 3:30; 2. Atomic Punk 3:00; 3. Feel Your Love Tonight 3:40; 4. Little Dreamer 3:22; 5. Ice Cream Man (John Brim) 3:18; 6. On Fire 3:01.

Notes: As stated on the original record label, "All selections written by Edward Van Halen, Alex Van Halen, Michael Anthony and David Lee Roth except as indicated." As noted above, assume it's the current lineup of the band writing the songs, unless noted, in which case it will be a cover. Also as stated, original lineup is: "David Roth – vocals; Edward Van Halen – guitar; Alex Van Halen – drums; Michael Anthony – bass guitar."

II

Released March 23, 1979; Warner Bros. HS 3312.

Recorded December 10–16, 1978, at Sunset Sound Recorders, Hollywood, CA.

Produced by Ted Templeman.

Side 1: 1. You're No Good (Clint Ballard, Jr.) 3:12; 2. Dance the Night Away 3:04; 3. Somebody Get Me a Doctor 2:51; 4. Bottoms Up! 3:04; 5. Outta Love Again 2:49.

Side 2: 1. Light Up the Sky 3:09; 2. Spanish Fly 0:58; 3. D.O.A. 4:07; 4. Women in Love . . . . . 4:05; 5. Beautiful Girls 3:55.

WOMEN AND CHILDREN FIRST

Released March 26, 1980; Warner Bros. HS 3415.

Recorded December 1979–February 1980 at Sunset Sound Recorders, Hollywood, CA.

Produced by Ted Templeman.

Side 1: 1. And the Cradle Will Rock . . . 3:11; 2. Everybody Wants Some!! 5:05; 3. Fools 5:55; 4. Romeo Delight 4:19.

Side 2: 1. Tora! Tora! 0:57; 2. Loss of Control 2:36; 3. Take Your Whiskey Home 3:09; 4. Could This Be Magic? 3:08; 5. In a Simple Rhyme 4:33.

Notes: Nicolette Larson—backing vocals on "Could This Be Magic?" Also, Eddie gets an electric piano credit and will be getting various keyboard and synthesizer credits moving forward.

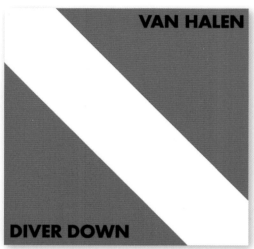

FAIR WARNING

Released April 29, 1981; Warner Bros. HS 3540.

Recorded March–April 1981 at Sunset Sound Recorders, Hollywood, CA.

Produced by Ted Templeman.

Side 1: 1. Mean Street 4:55; 2. "Dirty Movies" 4:06; 3. Sinner's Swing! 3:08; 4. Hear About It Later 4:33.

Side 2: 1. Unchained 3:27; 2. Push Comes to Shove 3:48; 3. So This Is Love? 3:05; 4. Sunday Afternoon in the Park 2:00; 5. One Foot Out the Door 1:56.

DIVER DOWN

Released April 14, 1982; Warner Bros. BSK 3677.

Recorded January–March 1982 at Sunset Sound Recorders, Hollywood, CA, and Amigo Studios, North Hollywood, CA.

Produced by Ted Templeman.

Side 1: 1. Where Have All the Good Times Gone! (Ray Davies) 3:02; 2. Hang 'em High 3:28; 3. Cathedral 1:20; 4. Secrets 3:25; 5. Intruder 1:39; 6. (Oh) Pretty Woman (Roy Orbison, Bill Dees) 2:53.

Side 2: 1. Dancing in the Street (William Stevenson, Ivy Jo Hunter, Marvin Gaye) 3:43; 2. Little Guitars (Intro) 0:42; 3. Little Guitars 3:47; 4. Big Bad Bill (Is Sweet William Now) (Jack Yellen, Milton Ager) 2:44; 5. The Full Bug 3:18; 6. Happy Trails (Dale Evans) 1:03.

1984

Released January 9, 1984; Warner Bros. 1-23985.

Recorded June–October 1983 at 5150 Studios, Studio City, CA.

Produced by Ted Templeman.

Side 1: 1. 1984 1:07; 2. Jump 4:04; 3. Panama 3:31; 4. Top Jimmy 2:59; 5. Drop Dead Legs 4:13.

Side 2: 1. Hot for Teacher 4:42; 2. I'll Wait 4:41; 3. Girl Gone Bad 4:43; 4. House of Pain 3:18.

Notes: Jan Van Halen—clarinet on "Big Bad Bill (Is Sweet William Now)."

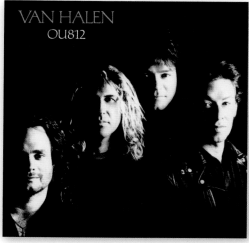

5150

Released March 24, 1986; Warner Bros. 1-25393.

Recorded November 1985–February 1986 at 5150 Studios, Studio City, CA.

Produced by Van Halen, Mick Jones, and Donn Landee.

Side 1: 1. Good Enough 4:00; 2. Why Can't This Be Love 3:45; 3. Get Up 4:35; 4. Dreams 4:54; 5. Summer Nights 5:04.

Side 2: 1. Best of Both Worlds 4:49; 2. Love Walks In 5:09; 3. "5150" 5:44; 4. Inside 5:02.

Notes: Sammy Hagar replaces David Lee Roth on lead vocals and as songwriter in the group writing credits.

OU812

Released May 20, 1988; Warner Bros. 1-25732.

Recorded September 1987–April 1988 at 5150 Studios, Studio City, CA.

Recorded by Donn Landee.

Side 1: 1. Mine All Mine 5:11; 2. When It's Love 5:36; 3. A.F.U. (Naturally Wired) 4:28; 4. Cabo Wabo 7:03.

Side 2: 1. Source of Infection 3:58; 2. Feels So Good 4:27; 3. Finish What Ya Started 4:20; 4. Black and Blue 5:24; 5. Sucker in a 3 Piece 5:52.

Notes: CD adds "A Apolitical Blues" (Lowell George) 3:50.

FOR UNLAWFUL CARNAL KNOWLEDGE

Released June 17, 1991; Warner Bros. 26594.

Recorded March 1990–April 1991 at 5150 Studios, Studio City, CA.

Produced by Andy Johns, Ted Templeman, and Van Halen.

1. Poundcake 5:22; 2. Judgement Day 4:41; 3. Spanked 4:53; 4. Runaround 4:21; 5. Pleasure Dome 6:57; 6. In 'n' Out 6:05; 7. Man on a Mission 5:04; 8. The Dream Is Over 4:00; 9. Right Now 5:21; 10. 316 1:29; 11. Top of the World 3:55.

BALANCE

Released January 24, 1995; Warner Bros. 45760.

Recorded May 25–September 2, 1994, at 5150 Studios. Studio City, CA, and Little Mountain Sound Studios, Vancouver, BC.

Produced by Bruce Fairbairn.

1. The Seventh Seal 5:18; 2. Can't Stop Lovin' You 4:01; 3. Don't Tell Me (What Love Can Do) 5:50; 4. Amsterdam 4:45; 5. Big Fat Money 3:51; 6. Strung Out 1:29; 7. Not Enough 5:13; 8. Aftershock 5:29; 9. Doin' Time 1:41; 10. Baluchitherium 4:05; 11. Take Me Back (Deja Vu) 4:43; 12. Feelin' 6:36.

III

Released March 17, 1998; Warner Bros. 46662.

Recorded March–December 1997 at 5150 Studios, Studio City, CA.

Produced by Mike Post and Edward Van Halen.

1. Neworld 1:46; 2. Without You 6:30; 3. One I Want 5:31; 4. From Afar 5:24; 5. Dirty Water Dog 5:27; 6. Once 7:43; 7. Fire in the Hole 5:32; 8. Josephina 5:42; 9. Year to the Day 8:35; 10. Primary 1:27; 11. Ballot or the Bullet 5:42; 12. How Many Say I 6:04.

Notes: Gary Cherone replaces Sammy Hagar on lead vocals and as songwriter in the group writing credits. Eddie Van Halen adds a lead vocal credit to his name on "How Many Say I." Mike Post plays piano on "Neworld."

A DIFFERENT KIND OF TRUTH

Released February 7, 2012; Interscope B001647702.

Recorded November 2010–August 2011 and January 2012 at Henson Studio, Hollywood, CA.

Produced by Van Halen and John Shanks.

1. Tattoo 4:44; 2. She's the Woman 2:58; 3. You and Your Blues 3:44; 4. China Town 3:15; 5. Blood and Fire 4:27; 6. Bullethead 2:32; 7. As Is 4:47; 8. Honeybabysweetiedoll 3:48; 9. The Trouble with Never 4:00; 10. Outta Space 2:54; 11. Stay Frosty 4:08; 12. Big River 3:52; 13. Beats Workin' 5:04.

Notes: David Lee Roth returns to the band on lead vocals and as a songwriter. Replacing Michael Anthony on bass and backing vocals is Wolfgang Van Halen. All songs credited "VanHalen/Roth," with VanHalen presented without a space for the production and mixing credit as well.

B.
LIVE ALBUMS

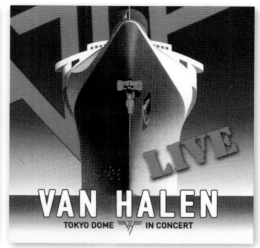

LIVE: RIGHT HERE, RIGHT NOW.

Released February 23, 1993; Warner Bros. 45198.

Recorded May 14–15, 1992, at Selland Arena, Fresno, CA.

Produced by Van Halen and Andy Johns.

CD1: 1. Poundcake 5:28; 2. Judgement Day 4:52; 3. When It's Love 5:22; 4. Spanked 5:08; 5. Ain't Talkin' 'bout Love 4:37; 6. In 'n' Out 6:20; 7. Dreams 4:49; 8. Man on a Mission 4:49; 9. Ultra Bass 5:15; 10. Pleasure Dome/Drum Solo 9:38; 11. Panama 6:39; 12. Love Walks In 5:14; 13. Runaround 5:21.

CD2: 1. Right Now 6:13; 2. One Way to Rock (Sammy Hagar) 4:58; 3. Why Can't This Be Love 5:22; 4. Give to Live (Sammy Hagar) 5:39; 5. Finish What Ya Started 5:50; 6. Best of Both Worlds 5:00; 7. 316 11:37; 8. You Really Got Me (Ray Davies)/ Cabo Wabo 7:58; 9. Won't Get Fooled Again (Pete Townshend) 5:41; 10. Jump 4:26; 11. Top of the World 4:59.

Notes: Live album featuring Sammy Hagar on vocals.

TOKYO DOME LIVE IN CONCERT

Released March 31, 2015; Warner Bros. R2 547643.

Recorded June 21, 2013, at Tokyo Dome, Tokyo, Japan.

Produced by Van Halen.

CD1: 1. Unchained 4:56; 2. Runnin' with the Devil 3:44; 3. She's the Woman 2:57; 4. I'm the One 4:12; 5. Tattoo 4:32; 6. Everybody Wants Some!! 8:30; 7. Somebody Get Me a Doctor 3:22; 8. China Town 3:22; 9. Hear About It Later 5:11; 10. (Oh) Pretty Woman 3:08; 11. Me & You (Drum Solo) 2:54; 12. You Really Got Me (Ray Davies) 5:34.

CD2: 1. Dance the Night Away 4:27; 2. I'll Wait 5:04; 3. And the Cradle Will Rock . . . 3:44; 4. Hot for Teacher 5:44; 5. Women in Love . . . . . 4:25; 6. Romeo Delight 5:48; 7. Mean Street 5:11; 8. Beautiful Girls 3:36; 9. Ice Cream Man (John Brim) 5:10; 10. Panama 4:21; 11. Eruption 8:08; 12. Ain't Talkin' 'bout Love 6:07; 13. Jump 5:48.

Notes: Live album featuring David Lee Roth on vocals and Wolfgang Van Halen on bass.

C.

COMPILATIONS

BEST OF VOLUME I

Released October 22, 1996; Warner Bros. 9 46332-2.

1. Eruption 1:42; 2. Ain't Talkin' 'bout Love 3:47; 3. Runnin' with the Devil 3:32; 4. Dance the Night Away 3:04; 5. And the Cradle Will Rock . . . 3:31; 6. Unchained 3:27; 7. Jump 4:04; 8. Panama 3:31; 9. Why Can't This Be Love 3:45; 10. Dreams 4:54; 11. When It's Love 5:36; 12. Poundcake 5:22; 13. Right Now 5:21; 14. Can't Stop Lovin' You 4:08; 15. Humans Being 5:10; 16. Can't Get This Stuff No More 5:14; 17. Me Wise Magic 6:05.

Notes: Compilation with two new Van Halen songs, "Can't Get This Stuff No More" and "Me Wise Magic," featuring David Lee Roth on vocals. Also included is "Humans Being," featuring Sammy Hagar, from the Twister soundtrack.

THE BEST OF BOTH WORLDS

Released July 20, 2004; Warner Bros. R2 78961.

CD1: 1. Eruption 1:43; 2. It's About Time 4:15; 3. Up for Breakfast 4:57; 4. Learning to See 5:16; 5. Ain't Talkin' 'bout Love 3:48; 6. Finish What Ya Started 4:24; 7. You Really Got Me 2:38; 8. Dreams 4:53; 9. Hot for Teacher 4:43; 10. Poundcake 5:21; 11. And the Cradle Will Rock . . . 3:34; 12. Black and Blue 5:27; 13. Jump 4:04; 14. Top of the World 3:54; 15. (Oh) Pretty Woman (Roy Orbison, Bill Dees) 2:53; 16. Love Walks In 5:11; 17. Beautiful Girls 3:57; 18. Can't Stop Lovin' You 4:08; 19. Unchained 3:29.

CD2: 1. Panama 3:32; 2. Best of Both Worlds 4:49; 3. Jamie's Cryin' 3:30; 4. Runaround 4:20; 5. I'll Wait 4:42; 6. Why Can't This Be Love 3:48; 7. Runnin' with the Devil 3:36; 8. When It's Love 5:39; 9. Dancing in the Street (William Stevenson, Ivy Jo Hunter, Marvin Gaye) 3:45; 10. Not Enough 6:48; 11. Feels So Good 4:32; 12. Right Now 5:22; 13. Everybody Wants Some!! 5:10; 14. Dance the Night Away 3:10; 15. Ain't Talkin' 'bout Love (live) 4:43; 16. Panama (live) 6:39; 17. Jump (live) 4:20.

Notes: Compilation with three new Van Halen songs, "It's About Time," "Up for Breakfast," and "Learning to See," featuring Sammy Hagar on vocals. These songs are credited to Sammy, Eddie, and Alex but not Michael.

Taking a bow at Cobo
Arena, Detroit, July 4, 1981

IMAGE CREDITS

b = bottom, L = left, m = main, r = right, t = top

Alamy Stock Photos: 7 (Chris McKay/Media Punch), 10 (dpa), 13 (Media Punch), 22b (Sheri Lynn Behr), 47 (Ralph Dominguez/Media Punch), 49 (Scott Weiner/Media Punch), 55 (Media Punch), 70t (Ralph Dominguez/Media Punch), 70b (John Barrett/PHOTOlink), 73 (ilpo musto), 77 (Jeffrey Mayer/Pictorial Press), 82 (Kevin Estrada/Media Punch), 84 (Ross Marino/Media Punch), 86 –87m (Michael Macor/*The Oakland* Tribune/ZUMAPRESS.com), 91 (Gene Ambo/Media Punch), 109 (Ross Pelton/Media Punch), 111 (Ralph Dominguez/Media Punch) , 112 (Jay Blakesberg/Media Punch), 119 (dpa), 127 (Gene Ambo/Media Punch), 128r (John Alashian), 132–133 (Jeffrey Mayer/Pictorial Press), 135 (Ross Pelton/Media Punch), 139 (Chris McKay/Media Punch), 140 –141 (Jeffrey Mayer/Pictorial Press), 142 (Jeffrey Mayer/Pictorial Press), 143 (Pictorial Press), 145m (Ron Wolfson/Media Punch), 146m (©Marino/Media Punch), 148–149 (Chris McKay/Media Punch), 151 (Gene Ambo/Media Punch), 152–153 (Aviv Small/ZUMA Press), 155 (John Angelillo), 158–159 (Chris McKay/Media Punch), 166 (Igor Vidyashev/ZUMA Wire), 167b (WENN Rights Ltd.), 168 (Derek Storm/Everett Collection), 170 (©Jerome Brunet/ZUMA Wire).

Robert Alford: 8–9, 18, 24, 25, 32, 33m, 50L, 50r, 51, 52t, 52b, 53, 129m, 130, 131tr, 131b, 164, 183, 192.

Kevin Estrada: 14–15, 28, 29m.

Getty Images: Front endpapers (Fin Costello/Redferns), 3 (Rob Verhorst/Redferns), 6 (Lorne Resnick/Redferns), 14 (*New York Daily News*), 17m (Michael Ochs Archives), 21t (Lynn Goldsmith/Corbis Historical), 30 (Gary Leonard/Corbis Historical), 31 (Michael Ochs Archives), 35 (Richard E..Aaron/Redferns), 37 (Richard E..Aaron/Redferns), 38 (Koh Hasebe/Shinko Music), 39t (Koh Hasebe/Shinko Music), 40-41m (Lynn Goldsmith/Corbis Historical), 43 (Richard E..Aaron/Redferns), 44–45m (Paul Natkin), 45b (Michael Ochs Archives), 59 (Michael Ochs Archives), 63 (Paul Natkin), 65 (Ebet Roberts/Redferns), 66m (Ron Galella/Ron Galella Collection), 67b (David Tan/Shinko Music/Hulton Archive), 71 (Rob Verhorst/Redferns), 75 (Ron Galella/Ron Galella Collection), 78 (Ann Summa/Hulton Archive), 81m (Paul Natkin), 82 (Steve Granitz), 88t (Aaron Rapoport/Corbis Historical), 103 (Marc Serota/Michael Ochs Archives), 107b (John Leyba/Denver Post), 108 (KMazur/WireImage), 114–115 (Jeff Kravitz/FilmMagic), 118L (Alaain BUU/Gamma-Rapho), 120 (Mirrorpix), 121tL (Rob Verhorst/Redferns), 121b (Rob Verhorst/Redferns), 122 (Kevin Mazur/WireImage), 125 (Jeff Kravitz/FilmMagic), 137 (Steve Granitz/WireImage), 138 (Robert Knight Archive/Redferns), 147m (Michael Hurcomb/Corbis Entertainment), 156–157 (Steve Jennings/WireImage), 167tL (Jeff Kravitz/FilmMagic), 169 (Jeff Kravitz/FilmMagic), 175 (Fin Costello/Redferns), back endpapers (Fin Costello/Redferns).

IconicPix Music Archive: 60, 61.

IMAGN: 88b (©P. Casey Daley), 89 (©Jeffery Salter), 161 (©Robert Scheer), 162 (©Tom Tingle), 163 (©Tom Tingle).

Lance Kovar/Frank White Photo Agency: 23.

Lynn McAfee/Frank White Photo Agency: 26m, 27,

Dean Messina/Frank White Photo Agency: 69.

Martin Popoff Collection: 20t, 21bL, 21br, 22t, 25tr.

Frank White/Frank White Photo Agency: 2, 36m, 56m, 68, 92, 98, 99, 100, 101, 113t, 113b, 171, 172, 173.

ABOUT THE AUTHOR

At approximately 7,900 (with over 7,000 appearing in his books), Martin Popoff has unofficially written more record reviews than anybody in the history of music writing across all genres. Additionally, Martin has penned approximately 120 books on hard rock, heavy metal, prog, punk, classic rock, and record collecting. He was editor-in-chief of the now-retired *Brave Words & Bloody Knuckles*, Canada's foremost metal publication for 14 years, and has also contributed to *Revolver*, *Guitar World*, *Goldmine*, *Record Collector*, *Lollipop*, braveswords.com, and hardradio.com, with many record label band bios and liner notes to his credit as well. Martin has been a regular contractor to Banger Films, having worked for two years as researcher on the award-winning documentary *Rush: Beyond the Lighted Stage*, on the writing and research team for the eleven-episode *Metal Evolution*, and on the ten-episode *Rock Icons*, both for VH1 Classic. Martin is the writer of the original heavy metal genre chart used in *Metal: A Headbanger's Journey* and throughout the Metal Evolution episodes. He also has a weekly podcast called *History in Five Songs with Martin Popoff* and is part of a YouTube channel called The Contrarians. Martin currently resides in Toronto and can be reached through martinp@inforamp.net or www.martinpopoff.com.

AUTHOR BIBLIOGRAPHY

Judas Priest: Album by Album (2024)
Iron Maiden: Album by Album, Updated Edition (2024)
Kiss at 50 (2023)
The Who and Quadrophenia (2023)
Dominance and Submission: The Blue Öyster Cult Canon (2023)
Wild Mood Swings: Disintegrating The Cure Album by Album (2023)
AC/DC at 50 (2023)
Pink Floyd and The Dark Side of the Moon: 50 Years (2022)
Killing the Dragon: Dio in the '90s and 2000s (2022)
Feed My Frankenstein: Alice Cooper, the Solo Years (2022)
Easy Action: The Original Alice Cooper Band (2022)
Lively Arts: The Damned Deconstructed (2022)
Yes: A Visual Biography II: 1982–2022 (2022)
Bowie at 75 (2022)
Dream Evil: Dio in the '80s (2022)
Judas Priest: A Visual Biography (2022)
UFO: A Visual Biography (2022)
Hawkwind: A Visual Biography (2021)
Loud 'n' Proud: Fifty Years of Nazareth (2021)
Yes: A Visual Biography (2021)
Uriah Heep: A Visual Biography (2021)
Driven: Rush in the '90s and "In the End" (2021)
Flaming Telepaths: Imaginos Expanded and Specified (2021)
Rebel Rouser: A Sweet User Manual (2021)
The Fortune: On the Rocks with Angel (2020)
Van Halen: A Visual Biography (2020)
Limelight: Rush in the '80s (2020)
Thin Lizzy: A Visual Biography (2020)
Empire of the Clouds: Iron Maiden in the 2000s (2020)
Blue Öyster Cult: A Visual Biography (2020)
Anthem: Rush in the '70s (2020)
Denim and Leather: Saxon's First Ten Years (2020)
Black Funeral: Into the Coven with Mercyful Fate (2020)
Satisfaction: 10 Albums That Changed My Life (2019)
Holy Smoke: Iron Maiden in the '90s (2019)
Sensitive to Light: The Rainbow Story (2019)
Where Eagles Dare: Iron Maiden in the '80s (2019)
Aces High: The Top 250 Heavy Metal Songs of the '80s (2019)
Judas Priest: Turbo 'til Now (2019)
Born Again! Black Sabbath in the Eighties and Nineties (2019)
Riff Raff: The Top 250 Heavy Metal Songs of the '70s (2018)

Lettin' Go: UFO in the '80s and '90s (2018)
Queen: Album by Album (2018)
Unchained: A Van Halen User Manual (2018)
Iron Maiden: Album by Album (2018)
Sabotage! Black Sabbath in the Seventies (2018)
Welcome to My Nightmare: 50 Years of Alice Cooper (2018)
Judas Priest: Decade of Domination (2018)
Popoff Archive – 6: American Power Metal (2018)
Popoff Archive – 5: European Power Metal (2018)
The Clash: All the Albums, All the Songs (2018)
Pink Floyd: Album by Album (2018)
Lights Out: Surviving the '70s with UFO (2018)
AC/DC: Album by Album (2017)
Led Zeppelin: Song by Song (2017)
Tornado of Souls: Thrash's Titanic Clash (2017)
Caught in a Mosh: The Golden Era of Thrash (2017)
Metal Collector: Gathered Tales from Headbangers (2017)
Rush: Album by Album (2017)
Beer Drinkers and Hell Raisers: The Rise of Motörhead (2017)
Hit the Lights: The Birth of Thrash (2017)
Popoff Archive – 4: Classic Rock (2017)
Popoff Archive – 3: Hair Metal (2017)
Metallica: The Complete Illustrated History, Updated Edition (2016)
Rush: The Illustrated History, Updated Edition (2016)
Popoff Archive – 2: Progressive Rock (2016)
Popoff Archive – 1: Doom Metal (2016)
Rock the Nation: Montrose, Gamma and Ronnie Redefined (2016)
Punk Tees: The Punk Revolution in 125 T-Shirts (2016)
Metal Heart: Aiming High with Accept (2016)
Ramones at 40 (2016)
Time and a Word: The Yes Story (2016)
Kickstart My Heart: A Mötley Crüe Day-by-Day (2015)
This Means War: The Sunset Years of the NWOBHM (2015)
Wheels of Steel: The Explosive Early Years of the NWOBHM (2015)
Swords and Tequila: Riot's Classic First Decade (2015)
Who Invented Heavy Metal? (2015)
Sail Away: Whitesnake's Fantastic Voyage (2015)
Live Magnetic Air: The Unlikely Saga of the Superlative Max Webster (2014)
Steal Away the Night: An Ozzy Osbourne Day-by-Day (2014)
The Big Book of Hair Metal (2014)
Sweating Bullets: The Deth and Rebirth of Megadeth (2014)

Smokin' Valves: A Headbanger's Guide to 900 NWOBHM Records (2014)

The Art of Metal (co-edit with Malcolm Dome, 2013)

2 Minutes to Midnight: An Iron Maiden Day-By-Day (2013)

Metallica: The Complete Illustrated History (2013)

Rush: The Illustrated History (2013)

Ye Olde Metal: 1979 (2013)

Scorpions: Top of the Bill (2013); updated and reissued as *Wind of Change: The Scorpions Story* (2016)

Epic Ted Nugent (2012)

Fade to Black: Hard Rock Cover Art of the Vinyl Agev (2012)

It's Getting Dangerous: Thin Lizzy 81–12 (2012)

We Will Be Strong: Thin Lizzy 76–81 (2012)

Fighting My Way Back: Thin Lizzy 69–76 (2011)

The Deep Purple Royal Family: Chain of Events '80–'11 (2011)

The Deep Purple Royal Family: Chain of Events Through '79 (2011); reissued as *The Deep Purple Family Year by Year (to 1979)* (2016)

Black Sabbath FAQ (2011)

The Collector's Guide to Heavy Metal: Volume 4: The '00s (co-authored with David Perri, 2011)

Goldmine *Standard Catalog of American Records 1948–1991, 7th Edition* (2010)

Goldmine *Record Album Price Guide, 6th Edition* (2009)

Goldmine <I>45 RPM Price Guide, 7th Edition (2009)

Blue Öyster Cult: Secrets Revealed! Updated Edition (2009); updated and reissued as *Agents of Fortune: The Blue Oyster Cult Story* (2016)

(2009); updated and reissued as Agents of Fortune: The Blue Oyster Cult Story (2016)

A Castle Full of Rascals: Deep Purple '83–'09 (2009)

Worlds Away: Voivod and the Art of Michel Langevin (2009)

Ye Olde Metal: 1978 (2009)

Gettin' Tighter: Deep Purple '68–'76 (2008)

All Access: The Art of the Backstage Pass (2008)

Ye Olde Metal: 1977 (2008)

Ye Olde Metal: 1976 (2008)

Judas Priest: Heavy Metal Painkillers (2007)

Ye Olde Metal: 1973 to 1975 (2007)

The Collector's Guide to Heavy Metal: Volume 3: The Nineties Ye Olde Metal: 1968 to 1972 (2007)

Run for Cover: The Art of Derek Riggs (2006)

Black Sabbath: Doom Let Loose (2006)

Dio: Light Beyond the Black (2006)

The Collector's Guide to Heavy Metal: Volume 2: The Eighties (2005)

Rainbow: English Castle Magic (2005)

UFO: Shoot Out the Lights (2005)

The New Wave of British Heavy Metal Singles (2005)

Blue Öyster Cult: Secrets Revealed! (2004)

Contents Under Pressure: 30 Years of Rush at Home & Away (2004)

The Top 500 Heavy Metal Albums of All Time (2004)

The Collector's Guide to Heavy Metal: Volume 1: The Seventies (2003)

The Top 500 Heavy Metal Songs of All Time (2003)

Southern Rock Review (2001)

Heavy Metal: 20th Century Rock and Roll (2000)

The *Goldmine Price Guide to Heavy Metal Records* (2000)

The Collector's Guide to Heavy Metal (1997)

Riff Kills Man! 25 Years of Recorded Hard Rock & Heavy Metal (1993)

See martinpopoff.com for complete details and ordering information.

First published in 2023 by Motorbooks,
an imprint of The Quarto Group,
100 Cummings Center, Suite 265-D,
Beverly, MA 01915, USA.
T (978) 282-9590 F (978) 283-2742

Motorbooks titles are also available at discount for retail, wholesale, promotional, and bulk purchase. For
details, contact the Special Sales Manager by email at specialsales@quarto.com or by mail at The Quarto
Group, Attn: Special Sales Manager, 100 Cummings Center, Suite 265-D, Beverly, MA 01915, USA.

29 28 27 26 25 24   2 3 4 5

ISBN: 978-0-7603-8644-6

Digital edition published in 2024
eISBN: 978-0-7603-8645-3

Library of Congress Cataloging-in-Publication Data

Names: Popoff, Martin, 1963- author.
Title: Van Halen at 50 / Martin Popoff.
Description: Beverly, MA : Motorbooks, 2024. | Series: At 50 | Includes
  index. | Summary: "Van Halen at 50 is the lively and stunningly
  illustrated story of the legendary rock band told through 50 seismic
  releases, appearances, and other milestones"-- Provided by publisher.
Identifiers: LCCN 2023050456 | ISBN 9780760386446 | ISBN 9780760386453
  (ebook)
Subjects: LCSH: Van Halen (Musical group) | Rock musicians--United
  States--Biography.
Classification: LCC ML421.V36 P66 2024 | DDC 782.42166092/2
  [B]--dc23/eng/20231027
LC record available at https://lccn.loc.gov/2023050456

Design and layout: Burge Agency
Back cover photographs: Robert Alford

Printed in China